Caring for Aging Parents

CARING for Aging Parents

Straight answers that help you serve their needs without ignoring your own

RICHARD P. JOHNSON, PH.D.

CPH ™
SAINT LOUIS

Copyright © 1995 Concordia Publishing House
3558 S. Jefferson Avenue, St. Louis, MO 63118-3968
Manufactured in the United States of America

Library of Congress Cataloging-in-Publication Data

Johnson, Richard P.
    Caring for aging parents / Richard P. Johnson
        p.   cm.
    ISBN 0-570-04689-0
    1. Aging parents—Care.   2. Parent and adult children.   3. Aging
parents—Care—Religious aspects—Christianity.   I. Title
HQ1063.6.J65   1995
306.874—dc20   94-39335

    2 3 4 5 6 7 8 9 10   04 03 02 01 00 99 98

Contents

Introduction

*Honor your father and your mother, so that
you may live long in the land the Lord your
God is giving you. Exodus 20:12*

G od places high value on the parent-child
relationship. He Himself specifies in the
Fourth Commandment that we are to honor our parents. In working out this honor, we sometimes find
turmoil. What exactly does this word honor mean in
today's world? What must we do to honor our parents? More to the point, how can we honor them
without dishonoring ourselves or our own families?

No other relationship in your life has this kind of
history. Your parents are the giants who ruled your
family of origin; from them you learned your initial,
and lasting, meaning of what it means to love. They
are the people who served as your counterpoint during your stormy adolescent years. They are the pil-
lars of culture who shaped you into who you are,
who provided the discipline that you craved and

despised. Here are the people whom you held in contempt at times while still loving them and seeking their approval.

There comes a point in your life when these important people—who have provided support and love for you—need your support and care. Roles change and responsibilities change. Where once you needed them, they now need you.

Few human endeavors offer more opportunity for spiritual growth and development than elder caregiving. This miraculous opportunity for personal spiritual growth can be an emotional tangle of frustration, hopelessness, and guilt. You can avoid that tangle by equipping yourself with knowledge of successful caregiving and aging, finding support for your efforts, and finally, depending on the help of God's Holy Spirit to inject your faith into the caregiving role.

In this book you will explore a technique I call "Christian Personality Powering" and find how to apply it to the elder caregiving relationship. Elder caregiving is a unique calling to serve God's children in a special way. You will depend on Christ's presence in your daily life. It is in serving that you grow. Yet you are called to honor, not to give yourself away.

The Need for Care Is Expanding

The medical community works overtime to keep

bodies alive—and it's succeeding. However, few mechanisms in our culture help family caregivers shoulder the sometimes awesome burden of care required by individuals whose lives have been extended through "medical miracles." The growing number of frail elders in our society is unprecedented in any culture and represents a grand experiment never before undertaken. The outcome of this medical and societal experiment is unknown at this juncture.

One result of this medical success is that family caregivers can buckle emotionally under the burden. I work in a large medical center where I routinely hear well-meaning, but sometimes emotionally insensitive, doctors blythly say to the family caregiver at the time of her parent's discharge, "Of course your mom will need 24-hour care for the foreseeable future."

This shock penetrates the caregiver like a driven spike. *How can I possibly do that? Who can help me? What will I do—I have a full-time job!* Fear cascades over the woman who has, without ever volunteering, just entered the ranks of the army of adult child elder caregivers. Her life will never be the same! Without the benefit of an orientation session, let alone any formal training, she awkwardly gathers herself up and heads into the great caregiving unknown. At this fragile point she has not a clue about the breadth and depth of the dramatic life challenge she faces.

A Few Final Notes
before You Continue

I will often use feminine pronouns to refer to both aging parents and adult child caregivers. While both categories obviously contain members of both genders, statistics tell us that the average woman will spend more time caring for her parents than raising her children. Demographics indicate that women live longer than men.

Throughout the book, I refer to *elder caregivers.* The term *elder caregiver* does not refer to an old caregiver but rather to any person—usually an adult child or spouse—who either directly or indirectly gives care and support to an older person. I like to refer to older persons as *elders* or *seniors;* these terms are more dignified than the commonly used term *elderly,* which I believe to be patronizing.

One doesn't need to give direct care to be a caregiver. Adult children who live in cities far distant from their aging parents can still be caregivers. They take this role if they *care* deeply about the welfare of their parents and expend time, money, and other emotional resources in support of their parents. Anyone who has an older parent or who "cares about" any older person is a caregiver. It is to these sometimes burdened, and many times unappreciated, persons that I dedicate this book.

Richard P. Johnson, Ph.D.

1

The Strain of Care

Now my heart is troubled, and what shall I say? "Father, save me from this hour"? No, it was for this very reason I came to this hour.
John 12:27

It happened again! As she pulled away from her mother's apartment complex, Carolyn gripped the steering wheel so hard her knuckles turned white. Why was it that each visit to her mother became a struggle with quiet tension, internal disappointment, and repressed frustration—all converging to undermine her intense desire to have a close, heartfelt relationship with her mom?

———

Carolyn's mother, now age 82, suffers from several chronic ailments, including osteoarthritis, hypertension, and intermittent angina. Carolyn is the second oldest of five children. Her older brother, Ted, lives in a distant city. Even though he seems concerned about his mother, he can't give much direct care to her. Her two younger sisters and one brother seem too consumed in their own worlds of family and work to take any active role in their mom's care. This leaves Carolyn to perform the lion's share. She takes these responsibilities seriously and handles them with efficiency. Yet her heart aches—sometimes screams out to her—with a desire to build a more intimate relationship with her mom.

Mom's life was not easy. With five children to raise and Dad away on business a lot, Carolyn's mom was clearly the center of the family. She organized everything and everyone. Carolyn remembers that the household ran with order and structure: scheduled chores, prompt mealtimes, church on Sunday morning. The rituals of living were engraved in Carolyn's heart and mind at a very young age.

Carolyn was Mom's helper. Carolyn was ever-present, side-by-side with her mom, assisting here and lending a hand there. Very early Carolyn took on household responsibilities with a competence and flair that earned the praise and admiration of the person from whom she craved it most ... her mom. They worked in practiced rhythm. They flowed together as if they were one. And as they worked, they shared themselves. Carolyn could say anything to her mother. Always accepting, always empathetic, always "there," Carolyn's mother was a paragon of compassion, understanding, strength, integrity, and faith. She was a mentor of grand proportion; Carolyn's mother was her confidante.

This wondrous sharing extended through Carolyn's adolescence and well into her young adulthood. Carolyn shared her life with her mother: her courtship, her wedding, her early married years, the birth of her three children, difficulties, joys ... everything. The closeness was good, fulfilling, comforting—until about two years ago. Carolyn noticed that her time with Mom began to lack something. As the months passed, Carolyn realized that her mom seemed strangely distant. She wasn't there for Carolyn as she had been.

Once a person who only seemed concerned for others, Carolyn's mom began to focus on herself. Her conversations became egocentric. She talked about herself—particularly her health or lack of it— and seemed to dismiss Carolyn's life entirely. Carolyn wasn't used to forcing conversation with her mom. She certainly had to inject her own issues into their interchange. The more Carolyn tried to push it from her mind, the more it would resurface again on the next visit. What was going on? What had befallen her mother to make her act so unlike her former self? Carolyn had lost her best friend and confidante; she had lost part of herself.

Carolyn grew to resent her mother for the apparently uncaring person she had become. Her mom started to become dependent upon her. At first Mom's requests were minor—stop at the market, get some stamps, run some errands. Gradually, her requests shrilled to demands.

Carolyn began to feel the first tugs of her mother's manipulation. Then came the day of the first big "blow-up," when Carolyn's frustration escalated into anger. The months of piled-up feelings gushed out in a barrage of emotion. It ended as quickly as it had started, but even so, Carolyn cried herself to sleep that night, vowing never again to let out her inner feelings. From now on, she would wall-up her internal tensions, close-off her confusion, and simply keep her feelings to herself.

Adult Child Elder Caregivers Need Support

Carolyn's story is not unique. Certainly the personalities are unique, but the themes of personal loss are all too common—dependency, emotional unrest, and intergenerational conflict between two people who share a relationship like no other. A growing myth in our culture is that families are selfishly abandoning their aging parents. After some 15 years of dealing with adult child caregivers, my observations are quite the contrary.

Families have cared for aging parents in the past, families care today, and God help us if they don't care tomorrow. The problem I see is not one of abandonment. Rather the major problem is the emotional press of wanting to provide all that one can while having only limited resources. Every caregiver at some time faces limited time, limited finances, limited patience, limited acceptance, limited knowledge, and—most of all—limited support for the caregiving role. Who genuinely understands the plight of the adult child caregiver, much less is ready to render assistance to her?

Numerous studies have researched the strain on caregivers and upon the care receiver. In every case, caregivers have been found to struggle tremendously. In most cases, this struggle is internal, shared with very few others outside of one's spouse and perhaps one's physician. These studies confirm, among other things, that caregivers are more at risk for ill health than are noncaregivers.

In a California-based study, Victor Cicerrelli reported that 27 percent of the adult child caregivers in the sample were emotionally exhausted as a direct consequence of their caregiving role (*Helping Elderly Parents: The Role of Adult Children.* Auburn House, Greenwood Publishing House, 1981). Fully 30 percent registered being physically worn-out by caregiving. And 75 percent claimed to suffer from significant negative feelings toward their aging parent. I'm inclined to believe that the other 25 percent were simply blocking or denying negative feelings. As you can see, the elder caregiving role is a stressful one indeed.

The Strain-of-Care Inventory

To confirm such findings, I decided to perform my own investigation. I devised an assessment with 15 questions designed to uncover the level and content of the stress that caregivers feel. Before you read this next section, which outlines the results of my national sample of caregivers, take the Strain-of-Care Inventory on the next page. Then compare your responses to the results of the national sample.

✏ **Directions:** Circle the number below each statement or question that seems to convey *best* how you feel about dealing with your aging parent right now. Where comments are requested, be as concise and accurate as you can.

1. What is the strongest *positive* emotion that you feel toward your aging parent?

_____

2. To what degree do you normally feel this emotion? Circle one.

    1   2   3   4   5   6   7   8   9   1 0
    low degree   high degree

3. What is the strongest *negative* emotion that you feel toward your aging parent?

_____

4. To what degree do you normally feel this emotion? Circle one.

    1   2   3   4   5   6   7   8   9   1 0
    low degree   high degree

5. What percentage of the time you spend with your aging parent does your positive emotion outweigh your negative emotion? _____%

6. What percentage of the time you spend with your aging parent does your negative emotion outweigh your positive emotion? _____ %

7. To what degree have you felt yourself withdraw from your aging parent because of negative emotions that you feel? Circle one.

1   2   3   4   5   6   7   8   9   1 0
low degree   high degree

8. To what degree has tension emerged between you and your siblings, or any of their spouses, because of disagreements over care for your aging parent (in-law)? Circle one.

1   2   3   4   5   6   7   8   9   1 0
low degree   high degree

9. To what degree has dealing with your aging parent (in-law) caused strain in your own marital relationship? Circle one.

1   2   3   4   5   6   7   8   9   10
low degree   high degree

10. To what degree does your aging parent (in-law) abuse you? Circle one.

1   2   3   4   5   6   7   8   9   10
low degree   high degree

11. Specifically, what forms does this abuse take?

_____

12. To what degree do you abuse your aging parent (in-law)? Circle one.

1   2   3   4   5   6   7   8   9   10

low degree   high degree

13. Specifically, what forms does this abuse take?

_____

14. To what degree has dealing with your aging parent affected your health either (circle one) *negatively* or *positively?* Circle degree.

1   2   3   4   5   6   7   8   9   10

low degree   high degree

15. What do you do to deal with the "strain of care" you feel as a result of dealing with your aging parent (in-law)?

_____

_____

Here's how the national sample of adult child caregivers responded to the Strain-of-Care Inventory.

Question 1 asked respondents to list the strongest **positive** *emotion they feel toward their aging parent. In order of magnitude, these were: love, concern, caring behavior, protectiveness, sympathy, respect, pity (?), empathy, compassion, gratitude, admiration, and responsibility.*

Question 2 asked for an estimate of the intensity of this positive emotion on a scale of 1 (low) to 10 (high). The average intensity of positive emotion given by the respondents was 7.24.

It seems obvious that this sample of caregivers not only loves their aging parents but also wants the best for them. They seem well disposed to honor their parents, willing and ready to shoulder the burden of care that is required. An intensity of 7.24 is significant and indicates that their care is motivated by a strong desire to give their parents the best they can.

Question 3 asked for the strongest **negative** *emotion the caregivers feel toward their aging parents as a direct consequence of the caring they give. Again, in order of the frequency, they were: anger, frustration, resentment, annoyance, pity, impatience, aggravation, guilt, sadness, distaste, and helplessness.*

THE STRAIN OF CARE

Question 4 requested the intensity of these negative emotions, which was 6.96 on the 10-point scale. Here we see a curious phenomenon. The very people who register strong positive feelings toward their aging parents are the same ones who feel exactly the opposite feelings. In statistical terms, there is no difference between 7.24 and 6.96. Statistically they are the same number because of the margin of error in any study. So what are we to deduce from such divergent findings? Caregivers feel internal conflict; they're confused and unfocused about their aging parents. At times they feel very positive, while almost simultaneously, they can feel very negative. This diversity seems paradoxical at first glance, yet it reveals the internal turmoil that is seen in caregivers' behavior.

Carolyn, for example, loves her mother very much, but at the same time, she resents how her mother has become abrasive at the very least and intolerable at most. In either case, Carolyn feels forced to be less than emotionally honest and direct with her mother, and she chooses to repress her feelings to smooth their relationship. This emotional reaction is very common and unfortunately sets up Carolyn for future problems.

Questions 5 and 6 are reflective of one another. Number 5 asks the percentage of time adult children spend with their aging parent during which they feel positive emotions. Number 6 asked the same for negative emotions. Adult children in this survey revealed that 62.5 percent of the time they spend with their aging parents, their positive feelings outweigh negative ones. In 37.5 percent of the time spent with aging parents, their negative feelings outweigh positive ones.

Once again we can see the conflict caregivers feel as they interact with their aging parents. How did you rate yourself on these two items?

Question 7 asked to what degree (1–10 scale) adult child elder caregivers withdraw from their aging parents: 5.93.

The withdrawal is not abandonment by any means. More often it's a reduction of the time spent with the aging parents, which caregivers may perceive as evidence that they are not doing all that they could. The emotional consequence of this *felt sense* of withdrawal is guilt.

Question 8 requests the degree of tension between the adult children and their siblings because of dealing with aging parents: 4.65.

Some of the most intense sibling rivalry I have witnessed emerges when Mom becomes frail. Disagreements can explode between siblings and lead to family turmoils that they have never experienced before. Such rivalry may take years to resolve and can cause stinging emotional wounds.

Question 9 asked the degree of strain in the adult child's marital relationship as a consequence of interaction with an aging parent: 4.84.

I have not yet seen divorces occur as a result of elder care in a family. What I have observed clearly is the strain that grows in a marriage when the couple is barred from enjoying social events or vacations. Each time they try to leave for an evening out, or especially for an extended vacation, Mom finds some reason for them to stay home. The general ploy is for Mom to fall ill the day before the vacation or, even more disruptively, the first day of the vacation. How many stories I have heard about weary caregivers forced to return from their vacation because they received a call saying, "Your mother has taken a 'bad turn,' and she wants you home just as soon as you can get here!"

Question 10 asks to what degree does the aging parent abuse the adult child caregiver: 3.65.

We hear so much about "elder abuse" in the media today, I wanted to document some of the feelings of caregivers when the reverse was asked.

Question 11 asked what form this abuse took, i.e., in what ways did these adult children elder caregivers believe that their own aging parents were abusing them.

Verbal abuse was the most frequently mentioned, followed by unreasonable demands, blaming, being bossy and sarcastic, expressing negative opinions, not allowing adult children any private time (including following them into the bathroom), vindictiveness, constant criticism, withdrawal, being ungrateful, lying, passive-aggressive behavior, and last, but not least, physically abusive behavior ... punching.

Question 12 asked to what degree the adult child caregiver abuses the aging parent: 2.11.

I realized that the response to this question would be skewed for two reasons. The first is that this sample of persons was rather enlightened about elder caregiving because they read the elder care newsletter that I write. Secondly, few persons admit, even to themselves, that they may be abusive to their aging parent. My purpose in asking the question was to compare the responses to questions 10 and 12. It was interesting to note that these caregivers believed that their aging parents abused them almost twice as much as they abused their parents.

Question 13 asks what form this abuse takes, i.e., in what ways did these adult children caregivers abuse their parents.

Again, verbal abuse ranked number 1, followed by, "I don't call her" neglect (in general), "I escape with friends," shouting, isolation (avoiding her), cutting back on visits, leaving early, arguing, I "ignore her," intimidation, anger, impatience, and showing disgust.

You can see that what these caregivers termed abusive was most often a form of neglect. No one admitted to physically harming an aging parent or withholding food, medical care, or other necessities of life. Caregivers believed they needed help in emotional interaction with their aging parents. The forms of neglect they listed were actually emotional reactions to the exasperation they sometimes feel. Such exasperation over an extended period of time, when mixed with other problems of living, can explode into full-fledged physical abuse.

Question 14 asked the adult child to estimate the degree to which caring for their aging parent negatively affected their health: 4.76 (1–10).

I have since documented in other research that the number 1 consequence adult children suffer from their care of aging parents is increased health problems. They report deteriorated health directly related to the caregiving role. The physical symptoms take many forms. The most common are head pain, back pain, neck pain, joint pain, insomnia, depression, anxiety, irritable bowel disorder, spastic colon, and general gastro-intestinal tract upset. This finding has been corroborated in many other studies.

Question 15 asked for ways that adult children caregivers cope with the strain-of-care they feel. This question generated a long list of suggestions—some apparently healthy and some clearly not healthy for caregivers.

In no particular sequence, the suggestions are: ignore it, call my daughter, take a day off, go to the opera, doctor gives me muscle relaxers, get out with her, talk on the phone, exercise regularly, quiet prayer, stay busy, limit my help, remember what she did for me, hire someone to be with her, talk to professionals, avoid contact, work on mutual projects, attend a support group, and finally, let my husband deal with it.

The Strain-of-Care Inventory offers some very usable insights into the pressures adult children caregivers feel regarding the role they have assumed. Perhaps the most illuminating and health-promoting response I have seen caregivers give to these results is a sense of relief that they are not the only ones who feel anguish about their role. It becomes obvious to them that many other caregivers feel like they do. Such an understanding builds connectedness and eases the emotional pain so often experienced by well-meaning and hardworking caregivers who are giving their all with so little appreciation.

What Adult Children Caregivers Need

The Strain-of-Care Inventory confirmed the work I was doing with caregivers and gave me new insight into an obvious need they had—a need I was not addressing. This insight prompted me, among other forces, to write this book.

The needs of adult children caregivers fall into two basic categories: information and support. Together, these categories create a safety net of stability and security that protects the caregiver from the ravages that elder caregiving often brings. Along with the steady help God's Spirit gives us in His Word, information and support can prevent an emotional and spiritual freefall into confusion, conflict, and self-criticism. Let's take a quick look at these two needs.

Information

Elder caregivers need information that allows

them to give the best care possible to their aging parents. The information also must enable elder caregivers to retain their own integrity, their own sense of self, their own identity, and not become swallowed up by the very care they are attempting to give. This type of information falls into six categories.

1. **Caregivers need to develop an understanding of the needs of their aging parents—and their own needs.** This understanding includes a deep sensitivity to emotional needs as well as the more easily recognized physical needs. Caregivers must recognize the role of loss in the lives of older persons as well as their common emotional reactions to loss. Finally, caregivers must realize that healthy adjustment to loss is mandatory for all older adults, including their own parents, and that they should not and cannot block these losses.

2. **Caregivers must learn to develop and strengthen truly healthy relationships with aging parents.** Such a relationship is the fundamental element of caregiving. It includes the three conditions of any quality relationship—genuineness, warmth, and unconditional positive regard—and mirrors the love and acceptance God has for us through the redeeming work of His Son.

3. **Caregivers need to learn how to break down barriers that may exist between the aging par-**

THE STRAIN OF CARE

ent and the adult child. Examining attitudes about aging and older persons in general is useful for the caregiver, as well as recognizing how myths about aging may be playing a role in one's caregiving. Perpetuating negative myths about aging is called ageism. When the caregiver identifies personal "hang-ups" about aging, barriers in the relationship with the aging parent are often removed.

4. **Caregivers must foster positive communication between themselves and their aging parents.** Caregivers can learn active listening and psychological attending skills—listening to the meaning behind their parents' words and offering empathetic feedback. Communicating empathy requires skills to reflect content and feelings.

5. **Sharing the love and the redeeming message of Christ's sacrifice for us helps aging parents and caregivers maintain a positive and meaningful attitude about themselves.** Knowing factors that contribute to "successful aging" and incorporating the notions of life stages and transitions into one's thinking are useful for both caregiver and parent.

6. **Nothing better prepares the caregiver and parent for death than Jesus' words to Mary, "I am the resurrection and the life. He who believes in Me will live, even though he dies; and whoever lives and believes in Me will never die"** (**John 11:25–26**). Knowing the five stages associ-

ated with death—denial, anger, bargaining, depression, and acceptance—helps caregivers and parents deal with death and grief. A hospice can provide support if the need arises.

These six broad areas of knowledge make up the core of what I believe caregivers need to know in order to deal comprehensively and confidently with their aging parents.

Support

The second need of adult child caregivers is support. They need to know, and even more deeply to "own," the concept that others care about them in their caregiving role. A support group can be vitally important in sustaining the caregiver. In our transient and sometimes impersonal society, support groups offer a forum for sharing oneself with others who, by virtue of their similar life experience, seem to implicitly understand the struggle we endure.

I have facilitated an adult child caregiving support group for the past 10 years. Each month I am drawn into the strain of care these wonderful people experience. I am indebted to them for two reasons. First, whatever I know about caregiving, I have learned from them. Secondly, they have opened up their lives and given me understanding that I have not experienced. Each month as I leave the support group, I feel an afterglow within me. I know without question that the Holy Spirit was powerfully present in our midst. The Spirit's guiding hand is so apparent, not only to me but to all the participants as we seek God's will.

Research has tried to explain why and how support groups generate growth and health. This research reports a number of benefits that support groups provide. Support groups offer mutual support in distinct ways.

1. **The support group experience provides empathetic identification.** I could individually counsel an adult child elder caregiver for a long time and not achieve the results that occur when she looks around the support group and recognizes herself in the story that another participant is relating about her caregiving struggle.

Another aspect of empathetic identification is the probability of immediate bonding. Mutual support also is given through problem solving. Participants not only share themselves but the problems they have encountered and how they tackled them with God's help. Support groups also aid crisis clarification. Some people come into a group and don't really know why they are there. What they do feel is a dramatically disturbing turmoil within them; they may not realize they are in crisis.

———————

One evening a woman joined our group and announced with no small amount of confidence that she had just "fixed" her caregiving situation. She had just moved her mother from an apartment down the street from her sister's house, who lived some 30 miles away, into an apartment down the street from her own house.

"Monday nights," she said, "are my 16-year-old daughter's nights to stay with Mom. Tuesday nights are my 15-year-old son's nights. Wednesday nights are my husband's, and Thursdays are mine. Come Friday, we start all over again!"

———————

This woman had no idea that she had just lit the fuse to a powerful explosive force within her family. Such an arrangement would, and could, never work for any length of time. Before the evening was over, the group—with very little help from me—had freed this well-meaning but confused woman from her desperate attempt to bring order to her mother's life by infusing turmoil into her own family. We cannot honor our aging parents by dishonoring ourselves and our families.

2. **Support groups provide practical education.**
Information passes around the support group circle
like lightning. Who got help at what place? What
home health agency gives the best service? Which
extended nursing facility has an understanding head
nurse? Where can you find help with medical care
forms? What hospital or doctor specializes in geriatric
care? The information sharing in a support group
never stops.

3. **Support groups increase the caregivers' confidence in their own God-given abilities.** Members help each other guard against over-working.
They assist one another in building their coping
skills. And they constantly confirm the directive that
caregivers must draw boundaries between their
own lives and that of their parents. Caregivers must
realistically identify what they can and cannot do.

4. **Support groups help caregivers grow in self-
affirmation.** It is easy to lose oneself in caregiving.
It's hard for caregivers to know what is normal and
acceptable in the role and what is "out of line." Support group members help each other by affirming
caregiving activities and behaviors that are healthy
and gently dissuading members from actions that
will eventually lead to sickness of any kind.

Information and support, together, provide caregivers a safety net of protection from damaging
themselves and their aging parents. They provide a

buffer between the rigors of caregiving and the possibility that stress could lead to physical or emotional strain that overloads and eventually crushes even the strongest person. Information and support are basic prerequisites for caregivers who want to prevent themselves from sliding into an emotional pit of uncertainty and confusion, which eventually could render them incapable of competent caregiving. A support group can be one tool the Holy Spirit might use in helping caregivers exclaim, "I can do everything through Him who gives me strength" (Phil. 4:13).

Even more than depending on one another, caregivers can depend on the uplifting grace of Christ, who, in His own dying agony, made sure His mother was cared for.

2

Caregiving as a Spiritual-Growth Forum

*She said to herself, "If I only touch His cloak,
I will be healed." Matthew 9:21*

A s I interacted with elder caregivers, I became increasingly aware of a curious
phenomenon. Some caregivers were *growing* as a
result of their elder caregiving. They were not simply coping with the situation; they weren't just
protecting themselves from strain of care. Instead
of being burdened by their increased responsibilities, they were growing spiritually and personally
as a result of it. They were becoming more alert,
more energetic, more purposeful—in short, more
happy with themselves, with their Lord, and with
their lives in general.

This observation intrigued me. How could it be,

I questioned, that certain people could become stronger as a result of their elder caregiving? What was different about them? What did they possess that many caregivers didn't seem to have? If there was some special ingredient, some magical talent, or some key to it all that they had somehow discovered, I certainly wanted to know what it was. I was determined to find out their secret!

I began a concerted effort to study these special caregivers. They were easy to pick out in a group. They were the serene ones, the ones who seemed to have it all together. They could offer counsel and guidance without seeming the least bit abrasive. They seemed experienced and knowledgeable, even though they had not been in the business of caregiving for as long as many others in the group. They seemed to radiate peace and strength. They inspired me!

I reasoned that whatever they had, whatever they were using to create this peace and internal calm, was certainly worth pursuing. Perhaps if I discovered their secret, I could even teach it to other caregivers. Wouldn't it be wonderful, I reasoned, to go beyond teaching basic coping skills and enter into a new realm of understanding? Could it be that there were some caregivers who actually used their responsibilities to propel themselves to higher levels of emotional growth and personal development? I didn't think so—not with my very real knowledge of human weakness and sin.

Whatever they possessed, it seemed to be beyond this material plane. They were supported by power beyond themselves that created a stamina of nonhuman proportion. They were very different from most caregivers in how they responded to their aging parents and to people and the world in general. They rarely displayed anger, dismay, or turmoil. They were concerned but not burdened, active but not frenzied, very caring but not overworking. They seemed to perceive the elder caregiving role through different eyes.

Christian Personality Powering

After years of observation, study, and research, I have concluded that these special caregivers possess the Spirit-given knowledge that God genuinely and profoundly loves them. What they have is the knowledge of God's love within them—that is their secret, the power and peace only God can bring. These were spiritually transformed persons, persons in whom the light of God's peace burned brightly. I found myself drawn to these people; something in them was like a soothing song to my heart. I wanted to know more about them. Caught in the stress of elder caregiving, what was catapulting them to ever-increasing reliance on God's power?

At first I thought these caregivers simply possessed more knowledge about God, more understanding of the Scriptures, more personal illumination of things spiritual. Over time I realized that this was not the case. They generally had the same knowledge as everyone else. What was identifiably different from most other caregivers was both simple and sublime. God's Holy Spirit had helped them apply their understanding and their knowledge about God to their everyday lives ... including caregiving.

These people of faith, through study of God's Word and the celebration of His sacraments, learned to see the Holy Spirit's power technique for injecting Christian learning into the very fabric of their personalities. Here was their "secret," the way they went beyond simply escaping from the turmoil and emotional confusion that can accompany elder caregiving. Their dependence on the faith and peace worked in their lives by God's Holy Spirit seemed to transform their caregiving into a spiritual development dynamo!

The caregivers that I observed didn't have a name for their spiritual growth. They didn't consciously know that they were practicing anything special; they simply did it. Theologians would define their spiritual growth and dependence on God's Spirit as *sanctification*. I call this marvelous transformation "Christian Personality Powering." I know that this is a rather psychological-sounding name, yet I think it captures the core of this life-changing competency found only in Christ.

As Christians, we believe that Christ came to this earth to be our Savior and Redeemer. His death on the cross and resurrection win us forgiveness and eternal life. God's Holy Spirit lives within us and empowers us as we live in God's will. What I call Christian Personality Powering is simply a way to keep our hearts and minds aware of the Spirit's leading. Here's how it works.

The Mechanics of Christian Personality Powering

Each of us has a personality—of that we are sure. You may like some parts of your personality, and you may wish other parts were different. But have you ever tried to figure out just what your personality is supposed to do for you? What are the functions of your personality? Most people don't have a clue. They live their lives assessing themselves and judging whether they have a "good" or a "bad" personality. Yet they really don't know what they are assessing. Consequently, they rely on others for evaluation rather than celebrating what Christ has done for and within them.

Your personality has a definite purpose. Empowered by the Spirit, it does a big job for you. Its primary purpose is to express the very essence of who you are to the world. Let's briefly define the six functions of the personality and then apply them to your caregiving role.

*The first function of personality is **belief.*** This is not belief in God, worked by the Holy Spirit, but your beliefs or feelings about yourself and the world around you. You have thousands of beliefs about your caregiving role—beliefs about your aging parent, about yourself, about the fairness of the caregiving role, the help you may receive (or do not receive), and on, and on. Your attitudes and beliefs form your belief core, your attitude structure, your value system. These three phrases refer to virtually the same notion—how you conceive of, make sense of, and give meaning to the world, all in the light of God's love for you and His will for your life.

*The second function of personality is **perception.*** You cast your gaze upon the events of your world in your own personal way. No one else sees the events of the world like you. In a sense, you project your beliefs out onto the world. The world teaches that "seeing is believing." Actually, when it comes to your own caregiving, what you believe is what indeed you will see.

The third function of personality is **thought.** After you have perceived in your own special way, you put data together, again in your own special way, and develop thoughts about what you have just seen. All this happens in a split second, so fast that you never even know what's happening until it's all done.

The fourth function of personality is **feeling.** Your thoughts are like automatic feeling-creation machines. Whatever you think will in turn generate corresponding feelings within you. Your feelings are "knee-jerk reactions" to what you're thinking. For example, if you think that the caregiving role is unfair because it controls your life, chances are that your feelings about caregiving will be negative, probably filled with frustration and sadness. On the other hand, if you think that caregiving is an opportunity for personal and spiritual growth, then you will probably have very positive feelings.

The fifth function of personality is **decision.** Once you have thoughts, you must choose what you will do with these thoughts. This is your discernment process; you can choose anything you want—no one is forcing you to make any specific decisions. But you do have all of your Father's help and support as you make your decision. You can prayerfully read His Word to discern His will and depend on His Holy Spirit's guidance as you make your decision.

*The final function of personality is **action.*** When you have gathered all you need from the previous five functions, it is time to execute whatever behavior you have decided is best for you. Your actions tell the people around you what you are all about. "You can tell them by their fruits" is another way of saying that your actions are the product of all that is you and God in you.

All of us use the six functions of our personality all the time. As you have probably already deduced from the brief descriptions, you and your Lord are in charge of how your personality operates. Christian Personality Powering means that you first become aware of how you have been using each of the six functions of your personality. Secondly, with the help of the Spirit, you work to transform each of these six away from what the world teaches about them and, instead, view them in the light of Christ and His Word. The next six chapters of this book take each function and analyze how you can shape that function to carry out the work of the Father in your caregiving role.

3

What Are Your Beliefs about Aging?

I am the resurrection and the life. He who believes in Me will live, even though he dies; and whoever lives and believes in Me will never die. John 11:25–26

M aria buried her face in her hands. Her tears broke through the barrier of her fingers and splattered on the floor. Maria was both deeply sad and passionately angry. Lately, when she visited her mom's small apartment, Maria found herself staring at her 84-year-old mother. She was struck by her mom's changing appearance. Had she aged all of a sudden, or had this transformation into disrepair been so gradual that Maria simply hadn't noticed it? Had she always been so sullen and withdrawn, or had she simply slipped into this emotional decay recently, perhaps as a result of the burden of her increasing physical problems?

Maria was overcome with emotion. Her mother's productive life seemed to be over. She couldn't even take care of herself. Maria was taking on more of her mom's daily life tasks—cooking, cleaning, shopping. She had long ago taken control of her mom's finances, such as they were.

Maria remembers the panic she felt so deeply on the day she found her mother's bills simply thrown in a kitchen drawer, some of them more than six months old. Why is Mother acting so irresponsibly? she thought. Why is she deliberately trying to make life harder for me? The questions that swirled through Maria's mind then were revisiting her now in all their unwelcome presence.

It became harder for Maria to live up to her own expectations. Maria thought of herself as the model daughter—ready, willing, and able to do whatever her mother needed. She had always enjoyed being with her mother. They shared, they laughed, they cried, they planned, they prayed together. Now things were different. As her mother aged, this kind of sharing seemed to be eroding away.

Maria tried to keep up the facade of their former relationship, but her efforts fell short as her mom focused on something Maria hadn't done or something Maria had done wrong. The Mom who had praised Maria as a good girl, a wonderful child, a trusted and dependable helper, even a gift from God, was gone. Affirmation was now part of the past.

But with the anger, Maria noticed a new emotion welling up within her. She felt increasingly sympathetic toward her mother. This sympathy engendered a protective attitude. Maria wanted to do everything for her mom. If Mom is aging, reasoned Maria, then she needs her daughter to be there for her. Day after day Maria first checked what her mother needed before she attended to her own needs. Maria became tired, frustrated, stressed, and increasingly irritable. Her mom's wishes became Maria's commands for performance. Maria rarely, if ever, questioned whether her mom's demands were necessary or even reasonable. She simply carried them out.

Today, Maria seemed to hit bottom. Emotional confusion enveloped her. Her usual methods of perseverance and sheer determination had escaped her. She felt alone, disillusioned, powerless, ashamed, and guilty. What had happened? Where could she go for help? Something had to change … but what?

Beliefs—The Core of Our Personality

The first function of your personality is your believing function. This includes all your attitudes, values, and beliefs about the world around you. Every action you take, decision you make, feeling you feel, and thought you think is born in, and springs from, a belief. You hold beliefs about everything. These beliefs serve as the primary motivating force for your life and direct your behavior in whatever direction your beliefs take it. Your beliefs are like huge magnets that pull you to action.

As a Christian, you depend on Scripture and the undergirding of God's Spirit to give you the knowledge from which your faith grows and develops. Here are nine core descriptors of the believing function of the personality, along with references from God's Word that magnify their meaning.

A belief is . . .

- Something you know for certain.

   > Jesus answered, "I am the way and the truth and the life. No one comes to the Father except through Me." John 14:6

- A personal state of certainty.

   > For I gave them the words You gave Me and they accepted them. They knew with certainty that I came from You, and they believed that

You sent Me. John 17:8

• A truth you hold at the core of your being.

> Be strong and courageous. Do not be afraid or terrified because of them, for the Lord your God goes with you; He will never leave you nor forsake you. Deut. 31:6

> Are not two sparrows sold for a penny? Yet not one of them will fall to the ground apart from the will of your Father. And even the very hairs of your head are all numbered. So don't be afraid; you are worth more than many sparrows. Matt. 10:29–31

• An idea at the base of your personality.

> Do you not know that your body is a temple of the Holy Spirit, who is in you, whom you have received from God? You are not your own; you were bought at a price. Therefore honor God with your body. 1 Cor. 6:19–20

• A statement that defines the real you.

> How great is the love the Father has lavished on us, that we should be called children of God. 1 John 3:1

• A spirit-given and deeply held conviction.

> For through the law I died to the law so that I might live for God. I have been crucified with Christ and I no longer live, but Christ lives in me. The life I live in the body, I live by faith in

the Son of God, who loved me and gave Himself for me. Gal. 2:19–20

- Part of your personal creed.

  Jesus said to her, "I am the resurrection and the life. He who believes in Me will live, even though he dies; and whoever lives and believes in Me will never die." John 11:25–26

- A life-guiding principle.

  My frame was not hidden from You when I was made in the secret place. When I was woven together in the depths of the earth, Your eyes saw my unformed body. All the days ordained for me were written in Your book before one of them came to be. Ps. 139:15–16

- A notion you value without doubt.

  Jesus Christ is the same yesterday and today and forever. Heb. 13:8

Just as we people of faith have firmly held beliefs regarding our Christianity, we have beliefs about aging in general and our aging parents in particular. These beliefs may not always be consciously available to us as we go about our daily lives. But they are at work within us, guiding our thoughts, decisions, and behaviors.

Here is a list of 10 common beliefs about caring for aging parents that I have found operative in many adult children. Maria was certainly ensnared by some of these. They continuously pushed her to do ... do ... do for her mother. The result of such beliefs is a paralyzed relationship between adult child and aging parent in which neither can grow (change) and dysfunctional behaviors are bred. I call these beliefs "disempowering beliefs" because they cause pain and make a person less effective. These disempowering beliefs terrorize. They are like hit-and-run raiders waging guerrilla warfare against the peace of mind of the adult child.

Disempowering Beliefs—Attitudes that Terrorize

1. **Aging is not good. It brings loss, dependency, nonproductivity, withdrawal, and decay.** We live in a society that is confused about aging. We are taught to honor people who are aging, yet our attitudes and behaviors tell a radically different story. We cannot follow a concrete prescription for living a life of wholeness and wellness in our later years because we don't understand what aging is supposed to be. We have no clear idea of what retirement will bring. We seem quick to support evidence that one's later years are bursting with potential; we point to any number of celebrated personalities who "remain active and productive" in the "autumn of their years." At the same time, we support early retirement as a "needed rest" in one's

golden years and generally patronize those among us who show the effects of this process called aging.

2. **Aging brings an end to emotional growth and personal development.** The fact is, our culture doesn't know how to react to older persons because we harbor antiquated attitudes about aging. Most of us can wait to be 90! Yet none of us register hurt, displeasure, or sorrow when a toddler develops into a child or when a child grows into an adolescent. We neither emotionally balk nor wince when an adolescent walks the developmental bridge to adulthood. Indeed we cheer these transitions that indicate health, strength, stamina, and a natural, normal progression of God's children.

Instead of regarding aging as a positive progression of growth, we view it as a slide into unfortunate disrepair. We mark growth in younger years in the tangible terms of height, weight, achievement, productivity, promotion, paychecks, power, and prestige. Growth during aging is less observable. It's more internal than external. It's more spiritual than worldly. It's more pensive than productive. It's more contemplative than competitive.

3. **Aging takes my parent's life away.** Down deep you wish your parent did not have to age. You want to protect him from the "ravages of aging."

You don't want to age yourself, and in some convoluted way, you think that if you can forestall, postpone, or evade the aging seen in your parent, you can control your own aging as well. You want to beat aging. Because you feel sorry for your parent and are helpless to reverse the aging process, you salve your sense of inadequacy by jumping to satisfy his every demand, a practice that is both unhealthy and impossible.

4. **I need to be the perfect adult child.** Within each of us lives the three-year-old self that sees the world through the vulnerable eyes of a child. This perspective is a psychologically primitive one, a fearful view that is ready at all times to flee from any situation that may interfere with the love that you desperately need from your parent. When you were very young, your primary need was for love from your parents. Consequently, you strove to be the best little person you could be. The giants that strode through your house when you were young were not supposed to be contradicted. What they said was true. What they said to do, for the most part, you did. That three-year-old is still within you, still urging you to "toe the line," still pushing for approval in the false notion that if you cease to receive such approval, you will suffer mercilessly.

5. **My relationship with my aging parent needs to be unchangeable.** It needs to remain what it

always has been. You seem to live by the philosophy of "peace at any cost." You will go to almost any length to avoid confrontation. You fear rocking the boat. You have a need to keep things as they are. You might even change big pieces of your life to ensure continuity of lifestyle for your aging parent. You are loathe to set boundaries for your aging parent, and rarely can you say "no" to your aging parent.

6. **I need to "do it all" for my parent. I must protect my parent**. You find it very difficult, if not impossible, to accept, let alone ask for, assistance from siblings, neighbors, or social service agencies. You think that no one else can perform the necessary tasks quite like you. Besides, you rationalize, Mom likes me to do it best. You complain about this fact to friends and family and even may harbor resentments about it, but you can't seem to change it.

7. **My parent's needs come before my own.** You have a tendency to place the needs and wants of others, especially your aging parent, before your own. In the words of one adult child, she "gave herself away" until she was "all used up." You depreciate yourself without even realizing it. You defer to the wishes of your aging parent, regardless of how illogical or unnecessary they may be. You seem to seek the responsibility for your aging par-

ent while you neglect responsibility for yourself. I will dishonor myself, you say, in order to honor my aging parent.

8. **My relationship with my aging parent can and should be great.** You can become emotionally lost in the depth of understanding and compassion you feel for your aging parent. You may seek meaning, purpose, and emotional depth in your relationship with your aging parent to an unrealistic and unattainable degree. You set yourself up for disappointment with unreachable expectations for your aging parent. You fantasize about what could be, when in reality that depth was never present in your relationship with your parent when you were younger. In all probability, it cannot be attained today. You futilely wish things to be different from the way they actually are.

9. **My parent must be right (even if she does seem illogical).** You become easily intimidated by displays of emotion—especially depression, fear, dependency, and anger—by your aging parent. Sometimes even the hint of disapproval, let alone a strong display of emotion, is enough to force you to give in to the wishes of your aging parent, however manipulative these may be. In extreme cases, just the thought of loss of approval will paralyze you into a nonassertive posture.

10. **I need to always be in control.** You feel things are

out of control, and you seek to inject order by attempting heroic acts of caregiving that usually backfire by overwhelming you. You then take out your irritation on the loved ones around you. Consequently, you feel guilty that you are not doing enough for your aging parent. This pattern is repeated time and time again until you begin to feel like a "bad" person and an unworthy child.

With beliefs, attitudes, and values like these, and similar ones that naturally flow from them, is there any wonder why adult children like Maria find themselves in perplexing situations? You may find yourself thinking that these beliefs are not like yours at all. I've had many adult children caregivers tell me that. However, I find that when they actually examine their behaviors, they recognize how "crazy" some are. They can only acknowledge that some of these are disempowering beliefs.

How do you change things? How can you turn around long-held beliefs about aging—something that you don't look forward to traversing yourself? Sometimes you aren't even aware of the beliefs. Beliefs are not easy to change. Like trying to quit smoking or losing weight, you have to galvanize the commitment from an extremely strong desire and a behavioral follow-through over a long time. Like any other life change, the starting point comes from awareness that change is necessary. Once this is accomplished, the job is half done.

Once you're aware of the need for change, you can address the beliefs directly. You can change disempowering beliefs when you clarify new beliefs to replace the old ones. These new healthy beliefs may be the opposite of the ones you hold now. The following is a list of 10 beliefs that have the power to transform the 10 disempowering beliefs listed previously.

Healthy Christian Beliefs

1. **Aging is a developmental challenge designed by God so you can learn better who you truly are.** Aging is a growth opportunity. Its purpose is the same as the rest of your life—to grow closer to God and to learn how to love others better. The worldly culture views aging as a tragedy, a senseless slippage into oblivion. Your worldly eyes see very little, if any, benefit from the maturation process called aging; consequently, you shrink from addressing it fully, directly, and functionally. You *can* turn this attitude around and recognize the spiritual value of aging, the gifts of aging, and the marvelous benefits that God intended for you. If you see this growth in virtue, you can transform the picture of your aging parent under the clear light of Christ's love.

"Aging to me has unpleasant aspects, but it is part of the pattern of life," said one enlightened caregiver.

2. **Growth and development of one's interior life over the entire life span gives purpose and meaning.** Aging unfolds God's grace in a way not seen previously. Where else but with aging can you learn virtues such as acceptance, humility, understanding, peace, patience, steadfastness, mercy, and justice? God puts you on earth for a purpose and under His Spirit's guidance, your journey brings you closer to Him. This path is littered with pain and loss, joy and delight.

You can call every aspect of life blessed if it brings you closer to God. Aging brings you closer to God as no other developmental stage can do. It's not because you are nearing the end of life on this earth but because you are challenged to learn from the losses that aging brings. Here is the truth, beauty, and goodness of aging.

3. **Aging gives life, it moves you toward your ultimate transition to eternal life.** Aging is not an ending process, but it can be best seen as a commencement of the grace we see at the core of spiritual development. A crucial point to remember when dealing with your aging parent or relative is that you are powerless to change the fact that aging necessarily brings loss. You, as an adult child, can-

not reverse the effects that aging has upon your parent, you can only address the emotional consequences of these losses.

You cannot bring youth back to your aging parent, or recapture lost health and vitality, or reverse a memory loss, or geographically relocate to be closer to your aging parent. You can, however, recognize your parent's feelings that result from these losses and gently reflect them back to your parent to let him know you care. You cannot change the facts of aging, you can only address the affective consequences.

4. **You are the adult child that you are; you have no need to portray yourself as anything other than what you are.** Being the mature adult child means that the accent is on *adult*, recognizing who you really are and "owning" your own unique personhood. The fact is, your Baptism has made you a child of God! As such, the Holy Spirit guides you as you live out the saving faith freely given to you.

At some level, the work that you perform with and for your aging parent is actually performed for you as well. It's a teaching device helping you learn how to love better. What you believe about the very purpose of your caregiving actions will have direct and dramatic effect upon you. Ask yourself, "What do my caregiving experiences teach me about the larger scheme of life?"

5. **Be open to God's healing power in your relationship with your aging parent.** All relationships require healing at some level. Even if you "get along" well with your aging parent and can genuinely say that you like and love them, there are always ways to bring God into your midst. There are always ways to deepen the spiritual connection between you and your parent.

I often find some perceptible separation between parent and child. This may be left over from childhood years, or it may have generated from more recent mutual judgments you have made about your mom or dad. This separation requires healing. Many times the healing process requires the adult child to learn how to be an adult—how to express her own needs, opinions, desires, and requirements, and how to equalize her own needs with those of her parent. In short, it's learning how to say no.

I hear some statements that tell me this process of learning self-trust is taking place:

> "I'm continually working on this—want versus need. Let the bricks fall where they must."

> "I think that Mother wanted to give up, move in

with me, and let me take care of her. Impossible! She and my husband never understood each other. It would be horrible."

"I no longer expect what cannot be. I merely accept her."

6. **Your goal is to "be with" your parent not be continuously "doing for" her.** What I mean by "be with" is not that you spend every waking minute with her, rather it means that you are emotionally "in sync" with your parent. You understand her feelings, her desires, her hurts, her dreams. You are responsive to her emotional level of being. A "doing for" relationship focuses primarily on the physical needs of your parent—is she taking her medicine correctly, is she getting enough nutrition, is she clean, is she comfortable—to the exclusion of the parent's emotional needs.

Certainly physical needs are important, but when they become the sole focus of the relationship between child and parent, the result is an anemic, resentment-packed bond. The relationship between you and your parent is the "honor" you share. Your only task is to be in relationship: You are her daughter or her son, and that's what you must be—always. Ask yourself what a good child is supposed to be first and foremost. When the relationship does not come first, the honor is leached out of the bond. What's left is only work and eventually, frayed emotions as these overly strained caregivers attest.

> "I absolutely ran myself ragged for two years, jumping to every whim, complaint, or wish. I finally learned that whatever I did was not satisfactory anyway. The disappointments were overwhelming."

> "I have to control how much energy to invest in caregiving. Obviously, I am not coping well with this."

> "I felt I was doing for mother what she should have been doing herself. I couldn't ask someone else to do what I considered an unfair burden to begin with. She was my mother and my problem. I don't think I complained to anyone except to my husband when I felt I needed to unburden my feelings."

7. **Love and honor your parents as your family and yourself. No one's needs are superior to anyone else's.** One caregiver dramatically expressed her desperation with her aging and infirm parents when she said, "They leave me breathless; they have taken every breath from me .... I have none left for myself." This unbalanced allocation of needs jolted this woman to rearrange the time and energy she was using with her par-

ents. It also pushed her to evaluate the core beliefs she was carrying around about what she was to be for her parents.

Many caregivers were conditioned in their childhood formative years to please their parents. This notion has become so deeply ingrained in their personalities that they resist efforts to dislodge the conditioned responses from their belief core. And when such responses are expelled, it is often with great guilt. These quotes are typical of caregivers who have not yet found a means to create balance and personality integration in their lives.

> "I still need or want approval, advice, counsel, comfort, etc.—those things that you may sometimes only get from a parent."

> "A long habit of trying to please those I love, my husband and my mother, has somewhat spoiled them. I am working now to break that pattern, which was not good for any of us."

> "Yes I do! I feel as though I've had enough. I neglect my daughter when she may really have a need. (She's 24 and lives 300 miles away.) She will call and say, 'Please come visit.' And I say, 'But Mom is sick right now. I will come soon.' That is one example."

8. You cannot force a particular type of relationship with your aging parents. You can strive to be yourself with them.

———>•<———

Faye, a capable office manager who successfully supervises 125 employees but who also is baffled and distraught by her own mother, was startled when I ended our phone conversation with "Keep your centeredness!" At first she was puzzled about the notion of personal centeredness. Even more confusing was the idea that she had her own interior core over which she had some level of control. She had never thought she might be able to exercise influence over her internal emotional terrain.

Faye was so extroverted that she allowed her mother, and her mother's actions, complete access to her internal tranquility. Faye didn't feel she could maintain an independent, personal, and private identity. In front of her mother, Faye was vulnerable, an emotional target, and generally afraid. To counter this newly discovered revelation, Faye made small reminder signs, "Keep your centeredness," and placed them in strategic places in her world.

———>•<———

9. Your parents are fallible; saying no to them is necessary, at times, in order to sustain an "adult-adult" relationship. Boundaries are an

important ingredient in every successful relationship. Respect is created by boundaries. The word
no is the means you use to establish boundaries.
When you somehow believe that the word no cannot be used, at that juncture you cease to be an
adult. In effect, you have become a slave to the
relationship. This is not what God means by the
word "honor."

Your goal is to establish and maintain an "adult-
adult" relationship with your parent. Adults express
themselves in their relationships, desires, wishes,
hopes, displeasures, heartaches, etc. When you
withhold your expressions from your parent, you
are relegating that relationship to something less
than what it could be. We all need boundaries, and
our failure to communicate our boundaries in any
relationship will result in the ultimate failure of the
relationship.

Here are two statements from caregivers who
have yet to establish and communicate boundaries.

> "My husband thinks I should take care of Moth-
> er. But he also thinks I should be 100 percent
> available for him and his mother. There's not
> enough of me to go around."

> "My mom expects things done 100 percent right
> and done yesterday. I just do the best I can and
> try to convince myself that's that."

10. God is always in charge. When you try to wrest power away from God by taking on the sole responsibility of the caregiving tasks, you shut yourself off from the power and grace God freely gives at all times. When you lament, "Where is God when I need Him?" what you're actually saying is, "I've cut off the avenues of grace that are my very inheritance as a child of God in Jesus Christ because I fear God can't take care of me and I'll be lost." This is the opposite of faith. You have made doubt your companion rather than love. The only consequences of doubt are fear and anger, two emotions that unenlightened caregivers unfortunately feel in abundance.

Here are three caregivers in various stages of healing.

> "I didn't want Mother living with us, and I didn't want her in a nursing home. I did everything I possibly could to make staying in her apartment work, even when she made no attempt."

> "Perhaps I do want to take charge too much, but if she wants my time, why doesn't she listen to my input?"

> "That is my inclination [to take charge], but I refuse to give into it—mostly!"

Conclusion

These 10 beliefs can serve as new attitudinal lights in the inner room of your heart that was formerly darkened by your disempowering beliefs. Take these 10 beliefs and place them, as Faye did, around your life spaces. Recognize them as your new way of believing, your new caregiving values, your new attitudes.

Whenever you find yourself questioning your caregiving role, stop to scan the first function of your personality. Survey the beliefs you are using as the basis for your behavior and your feelings. Ask yourself, "What would God have me believe in its place?" You'll be amazed at how this simple technique will empower and enable you to keep your centeredness.

Prayer of Caregiving Belief

Lord, help me believe. Help me understand that my beliefs determine what is real to me. I need to transform my beliefs in accord with You, dear Lord— especially my belief that if I give, then I will lose. My beliefs are the premises upon which I build what I accept into my mind. Help me purify my beliefs and reconcile them with Yours, dear Lord. I believe that in You is my strength to persevere. In Your name. Amen.

4

Perception: Is Seeing Believing?

For you were once darkness, but now you are light in the Lord. Live as children of light. Ephesians 5:8

Sarah closed the front door behind her. Her brow was furrowed, her hands were clammy, and her heart was pounding. Since her mother's untimely death more than a year ago, her father had somehow descended into a morose mood that was uncharacteristic. All through his working life, first as a junior and then as a senior partner in his law firm, he was always a self-assertive, determined, goal-oriented, and emotionally stable professional. If there were ever a person who called his own shots, it would be Dad. He was sometimes criticized for being too opinionated and even stubborn, but one thing was certain: Sarah never had to worry about her father's mental well-being. On the contrary, she always regarded him as the model of strength and absolute mental stability. Now all that had changed!

Sarah talked to herself on the drive home. "What should I do? I know I'll never get him to a mental health professional—he thinks they're useless. But I must do something, he's getting out of hand!" Indeed, Sarah's father was becoming increasingly irritable, unable to focus on the most simple of tasks. He even complained that television was "just boring." His sleep was disturbed in a way it never had been before. Sarah had to practically feed him because he was no longer interested in food. He had long since lost interest in his favorite leisure interests. Even his many friends seemed strangely absent from his life. Sarah would arrive at his place to find him simply staring out the window.

Her visits to her father increased as her worry deepened. This was starting to affect her health. Her husband, Jim, had remarked that she looked tired and that her own mood was not what it used to be. Sarah felt a deep gnawing pang of uncertainty that her father, a man she had always seen and depended upon as an emotional touchstone, had somehow descended into an angry depression, the proportions of which were unknown to her.

Where had this depression come from? Had her

father really depended on her mother without Sarah recognizing it? Where could she get the help that he needed? She remembered when her father had retired, she had seen some of the same symptoms, but they seemed short-lived.

Perhaps her mother had just smoothed them over. Maybe Sarah was seeing a cumulative consequence of her mother's death, added to his own retirement and all the other losses this hard-driving man had shouldered in recent years. His loss of status, the socializing with his co-workers, a sense of purpose in life, the time management that work provided—all these losses now seemed to be cascading over him in waves of emotional confusion and affective disturbance. Perhaps in some strange way, his very self-directed and pointed personality magnified the emotional reactions he was now experiencing.

What was Sarah really seeing? What were the true facts of the situation? She had always seen her father one way, and now that image was being completely altered. What was real and what was not? All these questions swirled in her mind and seemed to have no clear-cut answers. She was confused and uncertain because she wasn't sure what she was seeing; her perceptions seemed to have betrayed her, and it didn't feel good.

Perception: The Second Function of the Personality

The second function of your personality is perception—how you view the world around you. How many times have you been amazed that someone you respected viewed an event very differently from the way you had "seen" it. No one in the world views things the same as you do. It's one of the ways you are different from everyone else on this planet—you see things the way *you* see them.

When the apostles confronted Thomas with the wondrous news that Christ had risen from the tomb and was alive and that they had seen him, Thomas exclaimed that he would not believe until he placed his fingers in Christ's hands and his hand in Christ's wounded side. Here was a real skeptic who could not believe until he actually saw the event with his own eyes.

Yet, is reality only what you can see? Can you always trust your perception to be totally accurate? Was Sarah accurate in her perceptions about her father, or were her memories clouding what he had become now? Sarah was awakening to a new reality about her father and, consequently, a new way of experiencing him.

Much research has been done with the caregivers of persons with Alzheimer's disease. The researchers found increasing levels of anger, anguish, frustration, hopelessness, and other variations of emotional pain. The caregiver feels these emotions at increasing levels until something very subtle, yet extremely powerful, occurs—the caregiver shifts her perspective of the Alzheimer's victim. Instead of expecting "normal" behavior from the person, she lets go of the lens of yesterday and adopts a view of her loved one's actions in the clear light of today's reality. When this shift happens, researchers immediately see a dramatic decline in the intensity of the caregiver's confusing emotions. A change in focus, a change in perception, makes all the difference in the way the caregiver feels about herself. A semblance of peace is allowed to pierce through the bitterness of the Alzheimer's situation. A shroud is lifted from the scene, and the reality of abundant love can now bathe the event in a new and refreshing light.

We Perceive Events

Any occurrence in your life is an event. The event is a factual happening that includes your involvement. These are events: getting the mail, vacuuming the carpet, preparing a meal, meeting an old friend, mowing the lawn, giving a speech, getting a haircut, visiting your aging parent. A chance meeting is an event. So is a phone call, a drive in the country, dining out, or going to a funeral. With elder caregiving, an event is any interaction between you and your aging parent.

Events are, in and of themselves, quite neutral. An event is not good or bad, sick or evil, distorted or upsetting. An event is nothing and means nothing until you do something with it. The something you usually do is perceive it. You experience events according to how you see them, constructing a unique frame around the event. You make it a happy picture or a sad one, a good one or a bad one, an uplifting one or a deflating one, all depending on how you perceive it.

Seldom are you in charge of whether an event occurs. That's normally not in your power. Sarah's father will be as bizarre in his behavior as he wants—she has absolutely no control over that. However, she is in control of the way she envisions the events of her father's behavior. Her sight, coming from her "mind's eye," determines the degree that her father's current condition impacts her life. Sarah's perception tells her what is happening, as your perception tells you what is happening between you and your aging parent. If seeing is believing, then what are you truly seeing?

Perception can be described in many ways. Here are some words and phrases that may help you better understand how your own sight may lead you to conclusions and behaviors that may not be your choice. Perception is ... your own point of view ... the reality you see ... memories ... your awareness ... your observations ... vision ... what you witness ... what you behold ... what you visualize ... what you imagine ... your insight ... what you focus on.

As you can see (another perception), perception comes from you. No one else can give you a perception: They can share their own perception with you, but only you can make your own.

Disempowering Perceptions about Elder Caregiving

Your perceptions flow naturally from your beliefs about aging and the elder caregiving role. Whatever beliefs you have will be very accurately reflected in the viewpoints you adopt as your own. You become so attached to these points of view that you become unaware of the fact that you see things as you do ... it becomes automatic and unconscious. You believe certain things, and you naturally observe these things in the real world—indeed they become your world. You see what you want, and your beliefs and attitudes are what you "want." This may seem strange, but it's true. To a very large degree, you do create your own reality.

What reality have you framed about your current or projected elder caregiving role? Here are 10 viewpoints toward the elder caregiving role that I recognize in many caregivers—even those who want the very best for their aging parent. You may recognize yourself in some of these. Examine them and determine to what degree they "fit" you. Awareness of a problem is the first step toward changing it.

1. **I can see that elder caregiving has nothing to offer me personally.** Many caregivers see the tasks and actions implicit in the caregiving role as a rude intrusion into their own lives. They don't see any value in it, so they resist the very thought. They surround the caregiving role with the darkest of frames and see it only subtracting from their lives. They are blind to the growth and development that can be derived from the role. When seen through egocentric eyes, the caregiving role can breed fear and anxiety within the caregiver.

2. **I see my life revolving around my aging parent ... I have no life of my own.** Some adult caregivers can become so caught up in the needs and wants of their aging parent that they forfeit many parts of their own lives. It's not that they want to,

but they are genuinely unaware they are doing it until they break down into an emotional heap.

3. **I cither overestimate or underestimate the gravity of the problems that surround me.** This is a common problem among adult children. Adult children want the best for their aging parents, but they also feel sorry for them on the one hand and angry at them on the other. Thus adult children compensate for their own internal confusion. Either they blow things up so they can rush in and take over, or they minimize or deny problems in an attempt to exercise their unconscious hostility. Either way, they don't see the issues clearly. Sarah is a good example of both of these situations. Initially her past perception of her father caused her to underestimate his problems. Now that she has begun to recognize them more clearly, she runs the risk of overestimating them.

4. **I see my aging parent giving very little—if any—of the love and approval that I seek so much.** Each of us has that three-year-old deep within us. This little child only wants to be loved and accepted unconditionally. When our parent becomes dependent, having suffered so many losses associated with aging, he appears to be self-centered. The relationship between adult child and aging parent now shifts. The adult child becomes the nurturer while the aging parent takes on the

role of the needy one. Here's where we get the erroneous notion that roles have reversed. When this happens, the little child within feels rejected and left out.

5. **I don't recognize the times when my aging parent is acting in an unhealthy way—intolerant, abusive, manipulative, etc.** Sometimes it's easy to make excuses for the aging parent when her behavior is rude, or consistently irritable, or demeaning, or even abusive. Sometimes this is because adult children have grown up with this erratic behavior and have simply come to accept it. At other times, adult caregivers feel that they cannot point out their parents' negative behavior simply because they are their parents, and children don't have the right to call their parents out. In either case, adult children remain trapped inside their own barriers, unable to be honest with their own parents.

6. **I usually fail to see the positive side of my aging parent's personality.** Here is the perceptual block that widens the distance between parent and child. Because adult children pull a shade down over the negative aspects of their parents' behavior, they do the same thing to the positive parts of their parents as well. For years Sarah had completely overlooked her father's negative, bombastic personality, blind to how this behavior was really a cover for his insidious dependency. It wasn't until his wife's

death that this internal dependency blossomed into depression. Because Sarah denied herself perception of her father's depression, she blocked out the positive and more sensitive aspects of his personality as well. Again, she had no idea that she was doing this.

7. **I see aging as a downhill slide.** This perceptual distortion plays havoc with the parent-child relationship. Adult children who were formerly very close to their parents may pull away when they recognize that the aging process is making its mark on the parents. Because they are unconsciously afraid of their own aging, children transfer this onto their parents and squeeze the humanness from them. It's as if their parents were no longer full-fledged adults because they clearly show signs of advanced years.

8. **I see myself as limitless.** Sometimes adult children view their caregiving roles so seriously that they remove all limits from the amount and level of care that they can render to their parents. This irrational perception exposes the adult child to over-commitment and its attendant consequences.

9. **I see myself as selfish if I do things for myself.** Sarah's father became so needy that he tried to monopolize Sarah's time. His expectations of her presence and her service rose exponentially as his depression deepened. He wanted her there with

him every moment. If she tried to leave to attend to herself or her family, he would scold her for being ungrateful and thoughtless. When she tried to be honest (assertive) with him, she first endured his torrent of insults, then felt the avalanche of selfishness she heaped on herself.

10. I have an image that my aging parent will eventually change. Personality traits are rather stable over time. What your parent was like when she/he was younger will, in all likelihood, be the way she/he will be in later life ... only more so! When we closely analyze a parent's behavior that the adult child can't understand, we find it quite consistent with longstanding, but perhaps not so pronounced, behavioral tendencies. Yesterday's behavior and perspective are the seeds that grow into today's sometimes unhealthy behavior.

Christian Personality Powering Perception

The 10 perceptual distortions are common among adult children caregivers. These adult children are, for the most part, blind to the fact that they even "suffer" with them. They have adopted them without thought or discernment, and they maintain them through the same blind processes.

Your goal as a child of God and person of faith is to rid yourself of these disempowering perceptions because they create turmoil in your mind and heart. Here are 10 perceptual transformations. Please understand that the specific wording may not fit your particular situation exactly. Your task, should you want to do more than survive the caregiving role, is to comprehend the spirit of these 10 and incorporate them into your life to whatever degree you can.

1. **See your caregiving responsibilities as part of your journey toward wholeness and, therefore, holiness.** God has given you life. This life is precious—no matter what your own physical condition is. The tasks you are called to perform for your aging parent are also the same ones that call you to learn to love better ... your primary purpose on this earth. It's not that you forfeit your life to your aging parent, but it does mean you see God as your chief caregiving advisor. Under the Spirit's guidance, you are always learning how to be a better Christian, and the caregiving role is another step along that path.

2. **Recognize your Christian obligation to invest your talents in areas of your choice that may be different from your aging parent.** You are endowed with talents, interests, inclinations, and personality. As a person of faith, you want to bring these God-given gifts to the highest point of excellence. In order to do that, you must be diligent in answering the call to care for God's people but also

to bring yourself to new levels of being in the Lord. You cannot give yourself to the extent that you dishonor what God has deemed good.

3. **The problems that you may encounter with your aging parent can also light your path and help you develop vision.** The highest level of perception is to develop vision. Vision is the ability to see beyond earthly matters so you can gaze upon the things of God. The events of your caregiving role are neutral until you invest some type of meaning in them. An event is not a problem unless and until you see it as one. You can either get caught up in this world when you see events as obstacles, or you can grow spiritually when you perceive events as a means to shed light on God's reasons for your existence and purpose on this earth.

4. **Recognize that love is all around and is especially present in your relationship with your aging parent.** Dr. Gerald Jampolsky wrote a book titled *Love Is Letting Go of Fear.* I recommend it to anyone who is, as Dr. Jampolsky puts it, "trapped between the guilt of the past and the fear of the future." He reminds us that the only life we can live is in the present, and this is where love resides. Your job is to find this love in all its forms. He says love and fear are the only emotions; all others are variations or derivatives of them. Love cannot be experienced when you're fearful, and fear cannot

control your life when love is present.

5. **Clearly see any and all types of negative behavior from your aging parent as desperate attempts to request love.** Dr. Jampolsky holds that all behavior is either a statement of love or a request for love. This is a huge statement! It has the power to shift your focus away from seeing your aging parent in a negative light to one where you let God into the picture. Can you see the love in your aging parent's behavior, no matter how noxious that behavior may seem? Can you see the love in your own behavior?

6. **Vision helps you see all forms of positive behavior from your aging parent as displays of love and inner strength.** It's all too easy to overlook the good qualities of your aging parent—especially when your vision is clouded by the ever-mounting needs that he presents. Because of your emotions, seeing clearly is hard work, but it's work that pays handsome dividends. Your aging parent is simply reacting to his aging in ways that seem natural to him. You must see these reactions in his own context, not yours. Otherwise, you cut yourself off from the reality of the situation and sow seeds of discontent within yourself.

7. **Your relationship with your aging parent will change as you modify your perception of aging in general.** Many adult children seem to carry

around an idea that aging simply doesn't exist. Such a perception is actually a denial and bears no resemblance to reality. Aging happens all the time; it doesn't need your perceptual approval. Remain blind to aging and you only invite frustration into your life.

8. **Recognize the limits to your endurance and your strength.** It's not always easy to recognize the limits of your own stamina. If you are like most of us, you like to think you are capable of almost anything. This is particularly true in relation to your aging parent because you carry the attitude that you should do anything and everything for her comfort and pleasure. Burden yourself with such a perceptual frame, and you will push yourself beyond the limits of your endurance.

9. **Take care of yourself in order to maintain your own strength and stamina.** Remember that God's Word tells you to love God and to love your neighbor as yourself. Loving yourself seems to be the barometer of how well you can love others, including your aging parent. Give yourself permission to take care of yourself and you give yourself the physical and spiritual fuel to carry on your God-given function.

10. **Your vision of an aging parent is becoming more accurate every day. You see her much more clearly now.** It's sometimes easy to forget

that your parent is a person too. She has emotions, aspirations, hopes, cares, and wishes—just like you do. As you immerse yourself into the concerns of caregiving—regardless of geographic distance— you tend to de-personalize your parent. You can begin to regard her from a caregiving distance—to objectify her and not see her humanity. It's hard work to maintain a clear perspective when you are pummeled by demands, strains, and pressures, plus never knowing for sure whether you are doing the right thing.

Conclusion

Each of us develops our unique viewpoint as we mature. Our memories are the snapshots of our perceptions at a specific time. We carry many memories of our parents but are only aware of a few. What we behold today depends on what we beheld yesterday and what has been incorporated into our total experience. Our insight into our caregiving role is, in large measure, a compilation of our past experience. We decide what to focus on.

Prayer for Powerful Perception

Dear Lord, help me recognize that my perception is not fact but my choice of what I would like to see. By the power of Your Spirit, open my eyes to see my aging parents with a new perspective. Help me to see them—and myself—from Your loving viewpoint. Then help me to trust Your guidance and to truly care for my parents and myself. In the Savior's name. Amen.

5

Transforming Disempowering Thinking

Do not judge, or you too will be judged. For in the same way you judge others, you will be judged, and with the measure you use, it will be measured to you. Matthew 7:1–2

"Personalities don't change as people grow older," asserted the graduate school professor in gerontology (the study of aging), "they simply become more so!" Thus he summarized the often confusing picture of the bizarre behavior that aging parents can exhibit.

For example, Joyce was puzzled by her mother's lack of motivation, her inability to do almost anything, and her absolute refusal to try even the smallest tasks. Joyce laments, "I can't understand it. The sitting area in the nursing home is just around the corner from my mother's room. They show movies there each week. All she has to do is to take her walker 25 feet. Yet the more I ask, the more she refuses—she simply refuses to do it! Now, what can I do? I don't understand this at all!"

Expressions of confusion and disbelief are common among the most loving caregivers. When asked if the behavior of the parent is substantially different from behavior in younger years, the usual response is, "No, not different from the ways she used to be, just so much more exaggerated!" This is a truth that we, as adult children, must understand. Mom has not transformed her personality; she has simply modified it. More accurately, she has intensified it to the point where it appears to contradict the way she was. She has constructed a new facade over her existing face—a facade that confuses, confounds, and exasperates the best-intentioned caregivers. It seems that former nicks in the structure are now chasms. Blind spots become barricades. The personality has become magnified, sensationalized, and projected.

> Joyce seems more settled now, realizing that her aging mother is evidently not unique. But just as the slightest relief dawns on her face, she puzzles, "Why is it that only the negative

aspects of my mother's personality have become magnified? Why not the positive aspects as well?"

A good question! To answer it, we must look at the losses that aging brings: spouse, health, security, community stature, hearing and vision, appearance and body image, independence, a sense of usefulness, social status, involvement, and encouragement, to name a few.

The consequences of these losses are felt beyond the physical world and into the emotional one. The emotional consequences of loss are as dramatic, perhaps more so, as the physical ones. Emotional pain can manifest itself as depression, anxiety, fear, paranoia, guilt, rage, and in all sorts of personality distortions. These losses put great pressure on the aging personality and can cause the traits of yesterday to become the personality disorders of today. This is not to say that the aging personality can't mellow. Some positive traits can, in fact, become more accentuated and manifest themselves as wisdom, graciousness, tact, faith, and even celebration. As a gerontological counselor, I rarely, if ever, see these wonderful folks in my counseling office. However, I have great faith that they are out there in abundance.

Joyce seemed to settle into understanding, only

to be disturbed by another question: "But why is it that the negative aspects of my mother's personality seem almost exclusively directed at me? When there are other people around, she seems to be the most pleasant, gregarious, and charming woman. But when she's with me, she can behave like an absolute wicked witch." Another very good question—one that creates no small amount of guilt on the part of adult children.

Your aging parent may know he is acting differently. However, with whom can he feel more safe than with his ever-accepting adult child? Who else would put up with this disturbing behavior? Who has seen the progression from productive to faltering parent more clearly and more compassionately than the adult child? Then who makes the most obvious and convenient target for the negative emotions that the aging parent may be feeling?

In some families, there even swells the undiscussed assumption that, in some strange way, the adult children are responsible for the fact that the parent is aging at all! This attitude may be kept alive with statements such as, "I sure wouldn't feel (look, act, behave, etc.) this old if I didn't have you children to care for all my life!" Such a statement holds the adult children hostage to the myth that they caused the aging process that takes its toll and that they are expected to make up for this catastrophe.

> Joyce retorted, "Yes, that's exactly what my
> mother says, but why won't she help herself
> even when I'm not around? Why won't she
> entertain herself? She just sits there all day
> long."

We have now come full circle with Joyce's mom—we are now back to the original question. To answer it we must move to a description of one's thinking patterns.

Disempowering Thinking

Here are some words and phrases that can help us understand the third function of the personality, that of thinking. Thinking includes all interpretations, evaluations, judgments, understandings, criticisms, re-elections, considerations, deliberations, contemplations, collections of one's thoughts, and all assessments.

What thoughts rule your mind? Do they help to clarify, to illuminate, to bring peace—or do they continue the darkness of anger, uncertainty, and despair? So often we feel lost in disordered thinking that increases self-doubt, lowers self-esteem, and grows a cache of anger born of fear.

With the Holy Spirit's help, we need to train our minds to think the thoughts of Christ in all situations, especially the caregiving role. He calls us to live in this world but not to belong to this world. To accomplish this, we need to let go of those internal judgments that swirl through our minds bringing us nothing but separation and bitterness. Seek the Spirit's help to relinquish all thoughts that clutter your mind and sweep clean the disempowering thoughts listed previously.

It's not an easy concept to grasp, but with the help of God you can literally change your mind and alter the course of your life. You can get out of the judgment business. Your internal criticisms of your aging parent serve nothing. They only bring disharmony to your mind, confusion to your heart, and intemperance to your life. The only thing I request is that you judge, evaluate, and analyze the very process of your thinking. Your thoughts are not independent actors and actresses on the stage of your mind—you're the director of the production, as well as the lead character. You have the power to give them whatever dialog you want.

Here are the 10 most common disempowering thoughts I hear from overly strained adult child caregivers.

1. I think my aging parent shouldn't be changing.
Over and over, caregivers demonstrate this obviously inaccurate thinking. They seem unaware of it

and have no idea of the damage it has on their well-being. The elder caregivers' desire for security pushes them to keep things as they are. Psychologically, they want to be cared for and, therefore, wish their parents would stay as they were. This desire goes well beyond their typical search for the familiar; it penetrates to their core, the child in them wanting everything in place so that they can remain safe.

2. **I think my aging parent should do more—certainly more to help himself.** This thought seems to contradict the first. One would think that doing more to help oneself would bring about change. What many adult children really want is for their aging parent to do more to help himself so he can remain the same, retain the same capacities, keep the same health, perform like he always has. Even though caregivers know this is impossible, they seem to want the control to accept one form but restrict, or even reject, other forms. The list of activities that adult children want their aging parent to perform is endless: get more exercise, eat less (more), sleep less (more), get out more, interact more, read more, do more for others, pray more, be more pleasant to me, etc. The list goes on, and it has but one central goal ... the aging parent needs to stay the same as he always was.

3. **I think my aging parent shouldn't be angry**

with me ... should treat me better. Seldom do I find adult children who complain that their aging parent is too nice, too thoughtful, or too considerate. More common by far are the adult children who bemoan the sharp, thoughtless, and self-centered behavior they see in their aging parent. They can't believe their parent would feel any negative emotion toward them at all. "How can my mother be angry with me? Doesn't she recognize how much I do for her, how much I care for her, how much I think about her, how much I worry about her?"

4. **I think I shouldn't have any negative feelings toward my aging parent.** This thought produces more guilt in adult children than perhaps any other. It begins when the adult children realize disappointment with their aging parent's behavior, either omissions or commissions. This observation is real and accurate, but the adult child follows with illogical perceptions. The adult child perceives himself as bad, uncaring, spoiled, or self-centered because he has such thoughts about his parent. In effect, he is saying that he shouldn't have the thoughts he is having. Guilt flows generously from this irrational thinking.

5. **I think I must obey my aging parent.** Ex. 20:12 states the Fourth Commandment: "Honor your father and your mother, so that you may live long in

the land the Lord your God is giving you." Perhaps the most quoted commandment in both the Christian and Jewish faiths, it's also perhaps the least understood. As youngsters, the commandment echoed as a central theme in our religious instruction. To honor meant to obey. We were instructed to demonstrate faith in our parents as the legitimate representatives of God in our lives. In our small minds, our parents were God-like, and our religious training served to strengthen this perception.

6. **I think I must fix the situation.** Being good Americans, and having "can do" as a central theme in our cultural heritage, we naturally transfer it to every problem. Grounded as we are in our natural physical environment, we believe that all problems have a solution on the physical plane. Clearly, there is no solution to the problem of aging; certainly not on the physical plane. We all age, we all change, and we all encounter pain along the way. We may be able to retard the debilitation of aging, but we cannot fix it—without question it will continue. The solution to aging can be found only on the spiritual plane.

7. **I think I am responsible for my aging parent; it's my fault when things go wrong.** One thought pattern that erodes self-esteem is personalization—thinking that the unfortunate events in your aging parent's life, or even her negative feel-

ings, are somehow your fault. Your parent may allow you to "take the rap" for almost anything if you are willing. When you do assume responsibility, rightly or not, there is clear insinuation that you are somehow the cause of the problem or at least accountable to see that the problem gets "fixed." In time, your parent may come to believe that you are actually to blame. All this blame, fault, and judgment leads to guilt, the most insidious of all the emotions except fear.

8. **I think I'm not good enough.** Inaccurate thinking breeds more inaccurate thinking. When adult children think they are responsible for what happens to their aging parent—and that they must fix it as well—they set themselves up for failure. Naturally, they cannot fix everything—nor are they responsible for aging and its results. Yet the degree that caregivers think they are responsible is the same degree to which they will think they are not good enough. They create a spiral of internal discontent and emotional turmoil because they cannot achieve the results they desire.

9. **I think I know what's best for my aging parent.** At some point adult children shift their relationships with their aging parents and begin reversing the roles. There is a time when adult children provide parental nurturing care—sick care, food preparation, house cleaning, domestic decision-making,

and the like. Many adult children think they are parenting their own parents—yet this role reversal is simply a myth. They can never become their parent's parent. Nevertheless, adult children can come to think of themselves as parents and assume some form of omnipotence. This quickly extends to offering recommendations, advice, opinions, and directives—further damaging the relationship.

10. I think my caregiving work is never finished. Almost universally, adult children think that they need to personally give all the care their aging parent requires. An aging parent colludes when she refuses surrogate caregivers or, in extreme cases, actually fires helpers the adult child may have hired. This all reinforces, albeit negatively, the supposition that the adult child is not only the primary caregiver but the exclusive caregiver. When one person is the sole caregiver, the work is never done. Consequently, the adult child is left with loose ends that are never tied up and the charge of caregiving that cannot be even temporarily relinquished. Some adult children caregivers seem to handle this condition better than others. The more task-oriented, "a-place-for-everything-and-everything-in-its-place" kind of personality finds the state of continuous incompletion almost unbearable.

Christian Personality Powering Thinking

Your job is to replace your disempowering thoughts with ones that add power, strength, and meaning to the caregiving experience. The following 10 empowering thoughts can be the lights of Christ for your darkened mind. Give your thoughts over to the Holy Spirit. Train your mind to lay aside denial and accept the thinking of God as the most accurate thinking available—your true inheritance.

1. **Change is necessary and a part of the beauty of God's design.** Change is the watchword of the universe, as certain as the sunrise and sunset in God's creation. Change must happen. Even though you may not like the changes that come to your parent's life, they are part of God's larger plan. Take comfort in knowing that the God who created and controls change is also the God who knew your parent and you before you were conceived, who knows the count of the hairs on your heads, and whose grace is sufficient. (Ps. 139:13–16; Matt. 10:30; 2 Cor. 12:9.) He is a faithful God who sealed His covenant with your parent at baptism. Trust His love and care for him (and you) and seek His Spirit's guidance to lay the foundation for the work of love that is yours in caring for your aging parents.

2. **Judging your aging parent is the surest way to lose your peace of mind.** When you place a "should" on another person, you express an inter-

nal grievance against them; you are judging them to be wrong or deficient. Grievances will block you from truly loving another in the way God intends. When grievances and judgments invade your heart, they erode your peace of mind. When you hold grievances against your parent, a person you want to honor, the disturbance to your interior peace is even much more acute. Remember, it is natural for you to grieve the loss of security you feel at finding your parent is "not like she used to be." Take comfort in the fact that while circumstances change for you and your parent, God's love for you will never change.

3. **Your aging parent will vent negative feelings on you, but you need not take them personally.** It seems pervasive that aging parents do seem to dump their negative feelings (anger being the most prominent) onto their own children. Somehow they give themselves permission to express their true feelings in the relative security of the love of their adult children. Sometimes parents seem to think their children shouldn't be letting this awful thing called aging happen to them.

This emotional battering can be confusing. You bemoan your inadequacy in dealing with the situation and hurl your anger at yourself or those around you. Understand that it's common for your aging parent to feel the emotional sting that flows from the many losses of aging. You need not feel personally attacked when your parent assaults you with some of these feelings. Look at this obtuse behavior as a vain attempt to get rid of these feelings. This emotional projection is a common defense mechanism used by all of us, regardless of our age.

4. **It is normal, natural, and almost universal to have some negative feelings about your aging parent.** When her mother demanded something, Joyce felt constrained and even trapped into silence. On the surface, Joyce rationalized that her mother was old, and she should not upset a woman who was physically failing. On a deeper level, Joyce feared emotional reprisal if she were to express anything but compliance and adherence to her mother's wishes. Joyce's attitudes of "should" prevented the sharing that is so necessary in relationships. Her silence and nonassertive behavior robbed the relationship of closeness. Silence, which is so common among adult children, disables your relationships, accelerates your own aging, and denies you expression.

5. **The word "honor" means to hold in high esteem; it is an opportunity to show your love and respect.** As a child, you were taught that the Fourth Commandment meant you should obey your parents—and indeed it meant that when you were a little child. When you were a child you

thought like a child, and God gave you parents for a purpose: to teach, to love, to guide, to discipline, to keep you from hurting yourself and doing stupid things. You honored them by obeying them.

Change is happening, and now you are called to honor in other ways. By the very fact that you care for your parent, you are honoring her. Even more, as you assume the caregiving role, you honor her in new ways. Remember that this parent is a child of God, a vessel of the Spirit and, therefore, worthy of your continued care. To honor implies piety, a fidelity to your natural obligations and your duty to act in accord with the will of the Father.

6. **You cannot protect your aging parent from the losses that aging brings.** Some have described the aging process as a continuous reaction to the losses that it brings. You cannot stop these losses from occurring. You *can* address the emotional consequences of these losses. It's easy to forget this fact and proceed as though you somehow had the power to change the course of aging. Your intentions may be good, but this "blind protection" usually aggravates your parent and increases his dependence on you. Recognizing that you are powerless does not mean you are abdicating your obligations. Rather, recognizing you're powerless is the first step toward gaining some sort of control of the situation.

7. **You cannot take responsibility for your aging parent; only she can do that (assuming she is cognitively competent).** Unfortunately, personalization is an easy way for adult children to burden themselves. Joyce is a good example. Her thinking was that anything her mother wanted must be right and good, and more than that, any request made by her mother was tantamount to an order. Joyce seemed unable to separate her own needs and desires from her mother's. Joyce felt disturbingly "out of place" if she wanted something other than what her mother wanted and was unable to influence her mother in any way. Joyce was trapped by her thinking of self-depreciation. If you find yourself in that trap, assure your parent of your love but state firmly that you need to set some limits on your caregiving. You may want to talk to your parent's doctor, your pastor, a counselor, or even a close friend to help you analyze your feelings and set limits on your caregiving involvement.

8. **You are, without doubt, a child of God, worthy in every way.** You stifle your expressiveness and place unnecessary boundaries upon yourself when you try to be what others think you "should" be. These internal governors called "shoulds" and "should nots" actually force you to judge yourself and others as "not being worthy enough." This kind of self-inflicted judgment always brings sadness and sorrow. The renowned psychologist Dr. Albert Ellis

calls this thinking "shoulding on yourself," and he sees it as the chief cause of self-persecution. An example may clarify the destructiveness of this kind of thinking.

> Robert wanted the best for his father and always tried to honor him in a most genuine way. His father was a rather self-centered, controlling, and opinionated man who would inject his thoughts into any interchange. Robert had grown up knowing this about his father and even at times would take pride in his father's self-directedness. He marveled at his father's confidence and secretly wished he could have some of it. Feeling that he had always lived in his father's shadow, Robert harbored a constellation of negative emotions—fear, guilt, resentment, and envy among them—which remained unexpressed, unresolved, and unforgiven within himself. Robert lived on an emotional double-edged sword, on the one hand thinking that he should be like his father while on the other thinking that the negative feelings he experienced were testimony of his uncaring attitude toward his father. His "shoulds" and "should nots" trapped him in a vortex of pain and indecision.

What Robert and you need to know is that we can never be good enough or responsible enough to live up to any perfect standard—our own, our parents', or our God's. We are "good enough" because we have been bathed in the grace of God through the working of His Holy Spirit in our baptism. Our esteem and self-worth come not from what we do but from what Jesus loved us enough to do in our stead.

9. **Your best choices for your aging parent reside in a consensus of information and input from many sources.** You are not the font of wisdom for the overall welfare of your aging parent. Caring for an aging person requires much information and tremendous faith. One person cannot amass everything that is needed on the human plane and cannot distribute the necessary faith on the spiritual one. Consult every possible source of information and support that you can. Reach out to community and church resources. Investigate what's available, then learn new ways of thinking about the process of aging. Above all, pray, consulting the Spirit for guidance and heavenly strength in this time of change and challenge.

10. **Think of yourself as a care manager for your aging parent, rather than as a sole caregiver.** One of the primary lessons of elder caregiving is that you cannot do everything alone. Flying solo, as it were, renders you unstable and prone to crashing. Arm yourself with the latest data on caregiving support and resources, then assess your own

needs, desires, and capabilities and make decisions about what you can do and what you can have done by others. I'm reminded of a woman who had a responsible, full-time position at a large bank. After much soul searching and data collection, she recommended that her mother call a cab to get to her next doctor's appointment. For two weeks her mother refused to talk to her. The woman remained steadfast in her decision until, finally, her mother did indeed take the cab. Several months later, she overheard her mother say how independent she felt now that she was using the cab.

Conclusion

All thoughts are either statements of judgment and are therefore of fear, or they are statements of peace, joy, and connectedness and are therefore of love. We want to move from fear to love whenever and wherever we can. Forgiveness doesn't judge; it pardons. Forgiveness is born of love and sees reality most accurately. Forgiveness welcomes truth just the way it is.

Prayer for Transformed Thinking

Dear Lord, help me understand fully that You are with me always. Help me to order my thoughts according to Your plan, not my fearful plan. Save me from the guilt that initiates and maintains my disordered thinking. Give me the strength to let go of worldly thoughts and grab hold of Your thinking instead, so I may extend Your love. Take away the conflict created in me by the clash between the two thought systems—Yours and the world's. Help me always to choose Yours. In Jesus' name. Amen.

6

Understanding Your Feelings

"My soul is overwhelmed with sorrow to the point of death. Stay here and keep watch with Me." Going a little farther, He fell with His face to the ground and prayed, "My Father, if it is possible, may this cup be taken from Me. Yet not as I will, but as You will."
Matthew 26:38–39

Janet wanted to run away and scream. Once again, her 83-year-old mother had "jumped on her with both feet." Nine months ago, Janet and her husband had "temporarily" moved in with her parents to avoid placing her dad in a nursing home—a move they could not afford. Since then Janet's feelings had continuously "run away" with her. Her father was a dream to care for; his mixed Parkinson's disease and dementia had robbed him of intellectual capacities, but he was docile, compliant, and even appreciative in his own way. Janet enjoyed being with him and "doing for" him. Her mother, on the other hand, had hardened into a critical, demanding, utterly dependent person whom Janet tried to avoid as much as she could.

Janet felt horrible. On the one hand, she had very warm feelings for her mom, wanting very much to assist her. She loved Mom and wanted desperately to express it through her care. Janet viewed her work with her parents as a natural extension of the Fourth Commandment to "honor your father and mother." On the other hand, Janet could feel the cold and fearsome nature of an entirely separate set of emotions about her mother. She felt alone and angry, helpless and demeaned, controlled and avoidant, guilty and overwhelmingly frustrated.

Janet was in emotional conflict—a prime candidate for caregiver burn-out. Her ulcer was back, and she had developed arthritis in her knees and elbows. She felt exhausted all the time. Life had lost its verve and vitality; her husband seemed constantly irritable, and her own children, now all grown and on their own, would lecture Janet about how she was killing herself. They rebuked and pleaded: "Why don't you take control of the situation by putting your mother in her place? Why do you let your mother talk to you in that negative tone? Why don't you fight back?"

Fighting back, or even expressing her own feelings, had never been Janet's way. Janet's older brother and only sibling had held the spotlight so she always felt inferior. Her childhood memories of her mother hold the sting of criticism more than the warmth of nurture. She knew her father loved her dearly, but he never seemed to stand up to his demanding wife. He seemed unwilling, or unable, to find the boundaries that might balance the power in the relationship.

Janet's mother clearly held the reins of power in the family. It wasn't until now, when Janet ached for affection and support in this time of increasing need, that she realized the damaging imbalance that had existed in her family all along.

Age had magnified her mother's personality so that any spark of tenderness that flashed in Janet's memory had been crowded out. Like her father, Janet seemed incapable of developing a more balanced relationship with her mother. Since she couldn't resolve the situation, change her mother's behavior, even approach the situation directly, Janet's only coping behavior was borrowed from her childhood. She shut off her ears to her mother and retreated to a fantasy world of daydreams.

Where could Janet turn? She felt trapped by her inability to take charge and by the impossible costs of alternative care. Janet fit the graphic description given me one day by an individual who was consumed by his emotions. "Doctor," he said, "I'm emotionally circling the drain!"

Making Sense of Your Feelings

Adult children of aging parents are bombarded by recurrent and conflicting feelings to greater degree and depth than perhaps any other group. Understanding our feelings is a skill, yet we seem so ill-prepared to exercise it. Especially with our parents, we adult children who want the very best become tangled in our own emotional conflicts. We become paralyzed in indecision and confounded by the sharpness of our feelings. There must be a better way!

Feelings are a direct result of your evaluation of an event, situation, or relationship. You experience feelings on both cognitive and physical levels. You first *feel* feelings. Your body reacts to these feelings in many ways. Facial expressions and body posture are visible manifestations of bodily changes that are happening on even deeper (unseen) levels. Scientists now know that emotions actually cause chemical changes in the body. For the most part, these reactions go unnoticed.

Only when your feelings become so intense can you discern them or identify them for what they are. Janet may not recognize she is angry until she actually bangs her fist against the kitchen counter. She may not discern her fear until she feels perspiration. She may not recognize her elevated stress level until her hands begin to tremble. Feelings such as hurt, sadness, disappointment, helplessness, despair, and guilt are normally felt as a heaviness in the chest and can be accompanied by symptoms such as fatigue, lassitude, procrastination, difficulty concentrating, lack of enjoyment, sleep disturbance, and appetite changes. When left unclarified and unattended, these negative feelings lead to illness.

Feelings occur as a reaction to the thoughts you place in your mind. As we explore feelings common to elder caregivers, pray with David, "Create in me a pure heart, O God, and renew a steadfast spirit within me. Do not cast me from Your presence or take Your Holy Spirit from me. Restore to me the joy of Your salvation and grant me a willing spirit, to sustain me" (Ps. 51:10–12).

Some words and phrases that help describe the function of feelings might be: all joy … all heartache … all sentiment … all emotions … and all things of the heart. Whenever you are moved by something, inspired by something, or troubled by something,

you are operating in the fourth function of the personality—the emotional, affective function. Some
words often used to describe the feeling function
are: devout, burning, consumed, ardent, enthusias-
tic, zealous, sincere, passionate, eager, wistful, and
earnest.

Getting in Touch with Your Disempowering Feelings

Adult children who are emotionally fragmented...

1. **Feel guilty very easily because they think they
   haven't done enough.** Some adult children can
   feel guilty because they harbor secret and not-so-
   secret resentments toward their aging parents. Consequently, they feel guilty about being guilty. Sometimes they feel guilty because they think they are
   not doing enough. Sometimes they can become so
   overwhelmed by these negative feelings of guilt,
   frustration, helplessness, and fear that the very
   emotions horrify them. The guilt is paralyzing; it sti-
   fles and turns their world into a bleak landscape of
   self-doubt and eroding self-esteem.

2. **Often feel sorry for their aging parents because
   of the losses they have experienced and are
   befuddled by this increasing dependency.** Certain adult caregivers have difficulty accepting the
   increasing dependency of their aging parent, as
   well as the residual emotional dependency they still

have upon their parents. The dependency of aging parents is awkward because adult children remember them as self-directing people who went where they wanted and who did what they wanted. Now they seem physically and psychologically diminished. Adult children want the aging parents to be the way they were, but they know that this is an illusion. Conversely, adult children are almost stunned to realize that they remain emotionally dependent upon their aging parents for continued affirmation and approval.

3. **Feel neglected because they always wanted their parents' love but feel they never got it the way they needed it.** Caregivers can feel insecure about the love their parents gave to them. They may not have felt filled-up, nurtured, or affirmed as a child and, consequently, feel an emotionally empty place now. Presently the adult children have conflicting feelings. They sometimes feel resentful that their parents were deficient in giving the love they wanted. Yet they feel so emotionally needful that they will do almost anything for a chance to receive that missed love today.

4. **Feel confused by the personality changes their aging parents are beginning to exhibit.** To the adult children, the aging parents don't appear to be the giving, empathetic, warm, loving, and caring individuals they used to be. Instead they have taken

on a selfish edge, which is most disturbing. At first the children try to deny these changes. However, when they cannot be avoided any longer, the adult children begin to catch themselves in small acts of hostility such as forgetting something their aging mother asked them to bring, or picking her up a half hour late, or perhaps bringing her home earlier than usual. These may seem like small slips but not inconsequential ones.

5. **Fear rejection if they don't do what their parent wishes.** Adult children who are unfocused about their feelings will go to almost any length to avoid confrontation. They fear rocking the boat, feeling, instead, a need to keep things as they are. At times they even change big pieces of their own lives to ensure continuity of lifestyle for their aging parent. The little child within fears retribution from aging parents for all the transgressions it heaps upon itself.

Justified or not, the fear of rejection can crash through psychological defenses, wreaking emotional havoc and motivating the adult child to do more, and more, and more for the aging parent. The caregiving children find themselves trapped into wanting approval but fearing that it may be taken away at any time. If approval is withdrawn, the psychological three-year-old inside will be crushed. Naturally, this spiral cannot continue and usually ends in some kind of explosion between the adult children and someone they love. Interestingly, the explosion usually is not directed at the aging parent but at someone else.

6. **Feel low energy, emotionally or physically drained, or fatigued because of all the emotional strain.** If adult children don't explode, then they are at risk of imploding. Imploding is when the adult child turns personal negative emotions onto the self. Typically, this is when we see depression, anxiety, or psychosomatic physical illnesses such as headaches, backaches, or an irritable bowel. The adult child feels some form of pain that can be manifested in any number of ways. This pain is more likely changeable than constant. It seems to ebb and flow with the fluctuations in care requested by the aging parent. I have even seen adult children reach a condition I call total pain— where they are in pain on all levels: physical, psychological, mental, emotional, and even spiritual.

7. **Feel alienated ... feel they are different from other people because of their "strange" emotional reactions.** Adult children can assume that everyone in a group feels comfortable while they themselves are in pain. This feeling of uncertainty and alienation stems from the fact that they are unable to express their pain. The assumption that they are somehow different—an illusionary notion

at best—is self-fulfilling because feelings direct decisions. If one feels like a jerk, one must be a jerk. Such thinking-feeling patterns are destructive at their base. As a result, some adult children become isolated; to operate in a group—any group—they have to put on a mask. It is hard for these people to believe that acceptance does not have to be earned as proof that they are "good enough."

8. **Feel emotionally paralyzed, feel they cannot show their true feelings.** Some adult children become so adept at putting on their emotional mask that they lose touch with their true emotions and feelings—an emotional paralysis so deep that they block the feelings from even being felt. If this condition persists, the adult children appear stilted and rigid without being aware of it. Their ability to have fun, to enjoy the essential pleasures of life, ebbs until they become automatons.

9. **Feel like they're in the middle—all alone because there frequently is no one else to help.** Without realizing how it happened, some adult caregivers suddenly discover themselves in the middle. They have maneuvered themselves between:

1. Their aging parents and the community/neighborhood

2. Their aging parents and their own spouses

3. Their aging parents and their own children

4. Their aging parents and their siblings

5. Their own spouse and their children

6. Their aging parents and their parents' other caregivers (doctors, nurses, housekeepers, etc)

This is a lonely place. Whatever one does, it's bound to be wrong in someone's eyes. Consequently, someone is always angry or upset with the caregiver, leading the adult child to take a defensive or an apologetic posture toward almost everything. The result: The adult child gets sick!

10. **Feel easily intimidated by displays of anger from their parents.** Taking the mental stance that the aging parents must be right, or if they want something, it must be good for them, or that "I should get it for them," leaves the adult child open for large amounts of disapproval. Even the hint of this disapproval—let alone anger—is enough to make the adult child capitulate. In extreme cases, just the thought of disapproval will paralyze the adult child.

Christian Personality Powering Feelings

To be an emotionally enlightened Christian caregiver means that you depend on God to help you address the concerns and needs of your aging parent. The most fruitful way is to replace the 10 worldly feelings with affirmations that are extensions of love. From a psychological standpoint, it is much more effective to stand for something than it is to fight against something. Being for something is energizing while fighting depletes you. Rather than trying to block the debilitating impact of these 10 disempowering feelings or fighting to flush them from you heart and mind, take the offensive and formulate what you stand for, what you believe, as an enlightened Christian caregiver.

The following are 10 personal affirmations, each an affective replacement for the erroneous emotions described previously. Each is a spiritual antidote for the negative feelings that rob you of your peace of mind. Make these 10 part of your daily journey, especially your caregiving tasks.

1. **As a child of God, I feel clean and innocent knowing that God in Christ forgives my caregiving mistakes.** Certainly you, as a caregiver, make mistakes. You can offend your aging parents and yourself by what you do and by what you fail to do. You can do too much ... you can react in anger ... you can harbor horrible thoughts ... you can create problems through criticism, manipulation, and even jealousy ... you can forget the needs of your aging parents ... you can refrain from calling ... you can neglect your emotional needs ... you can even abuse the privilege of being a caregiver.

Yet, as a person of faith and by virtue of your Baptism, you are indeed a child of God. Trust His Word that "If we confess our sins, He is faithful and just and will forgive us our sins and purify us from all unrighteousness" (1 John 1:9). In Christ, you are forgiven. That is a promise. When you feel guilt— and the internal turmoil that it causes—take this as an opportunity for spiritual development. Ask the Holy Spirit to guide you in reviewing the basics of your Christian faith, including worship and participation in the Lord's Supper.

2. **I feel empathetic toward my aging parent and confident that God will give me the strength to do what is necessary.** "Feeling sorry" is perhaps the most destructive emotion a caregiver can feel. It drains your energy. More than that, it manipulates you to take on tasks that are clearly beyond the needs or best interests of your aging parent. Feeling sorry for your aging parent will cause you to over-commit and overindulge your parent. When you do this consistently, you send a psychological message to your parent that he or she is incapable on the one hand but entitled to this type of service on the other. This sets up an unrealistic atmosphere where you find yourself "running" ever faster in vain attempts to do everything for your aging parent.

Empathy and confidence, both parts of our Christian heritage, provide the emotional antidotes. To be empathetic is to understand the affective condition and motivation behind the actions your parent may use. It means putting your own judgmental thoughts and feelings aside and focusing only on what your aging parent is feeling. Whenever you feel sorry or befuddled, focus on the feelings your aging parent is experiencing at the moment and reflect these back to him. You will find that the sting of accusations, sadness, or fear is transformed to peace, love, and understanding. It's almost miraculous!

3. **I feel privileged and blessed to have the opportunity to experience love in this unique way.** Love is the only thing that multiplies when it is given away. There are many, perhaps innumerable, ways of showing love. It's important that you can see the way your parent is showing her love to you right now. You may not choose the same way to show love, indeed you may think this is a very strange way for your parent to show it! Nevertheless, that is what's happening.

Dr. Gerald Jampolsky asserts that all behavior— every action that you or anyone else engages in—is either a statement of love or a request for love. When you apply this concept to the behavior of your aging parent, you can start to recognize that what looks to be noxious behavior is merely a distorted way of requesting love. Practice this personal affirmation and you'll begin to know you are privileged for the opportunity of love and blessing that the caregiving task brings. It will reveal to you a deeper understanding of God's caregiving love for His children.

4. **I feel at peace that God's plan is at work in the relationship between me and my parent.** Aging is part of God's design; certainly no human mind can grasp the spiritual journey in God's plan for maturation. It's easy to shake your head in disappointment at some behaviors, the personality changes, or physical deterioration you lament in your aging parent. Yet here is God's plan, God's design, at work. What's happening is not destruction but transformation. Your parent is on the road that leads beyond form, beyond the physical, to a place where he will see God. Likewise, you are party to this marvelous process, with all its confusion, turmoil, and harshness. The caregiving role makes you a partner in this journey toward God.

> But our citizenship is in heaven. And we eagerly await a Savior from there, the Lord Jesus Christ, who, by the power that enables Him to bring everything under His control, will transform our lowly bodies so that they will be like His glorious body. Phil. 3:20–21

5. **I feel secure knowing that I will always have my parent's love to the degree he/she can**

show that love. Each of God's children has a different capacity for demonstrating love. Some personalities show their feelings smoothly and easily. Others tend to hide their feelings, and still others limit the kinds of emotion they can show—maybe only angry feelings or only positive ones. But everyone shows their feelings to the extent they can at the moment. Your parent, dealing with the losses of aging, can become somewhat hardened in her outward expressions of emotion, especially positive, love-related emotion. She may have come from a family that was deficient in teaching her how to show feelings. As an enlightened caregiver, you can always feel secure, knowing that your parent is showing the love, however veiled it may be, that she has for you.

6. **I feel vibrant and vital knowing that I am keeping the Fourth Commandment.** The Fourth Commandment is the only one of the 10 that gives a promise. When you honor your father and mother, your life will be long. This promise accents the magnitude of the commandment. When you consider that Jesus cared so much for His own earthly mother, even giving instruction from the cross for her care, you begin to comprehend the value of elder care and the rewards it offers. Ask the Holy Spirit to guide you, deepening your faith, and giving you peace in the understanding that you are responding to God's call to honor your parents—

going beyond what you should do or what you feel like doing.

7. I feel secure and whole in the knowledge that I am, without question, a member of God's holy family of faith. You are not alone in your caregiving responsibilities—I assure you from my own experiences. The thought goes even further: You are part of a larger whole, a holy culture of God's children, that engenders a wonderful feeling of connectedness. True wholeness is when all parts are unified according to central organizing principles. True wholeness is holy. There is surety and security in the bond between the adult child caregiver and the Spirit that becomes more clear and more present when the tasks of caregiving are seen in the light of the Lord.

8. I feel free to express my true feelings honestly. Adult children can experience contradictory feelings at the same time. Simultaneously they can feel love and anger, compassion and resentment, positive regard and disappointment. While they seem like paradoxes, these feelings need not emotionally destabilize you. On your path to becoming an enlightened caregiver, see your efforts as keeping with a higher order. Understanding that, you can become more warm in your manner, genuine in your expressions, and transparent in your motivations. As you come to understand your own feelings and where they come from, you can be more honest in expressing them.

Share your feelings (certainly not without license) with grace and care, but express them. Know that if you are not emotionally honest, that if you do not express your feelings as directly as possible, you are at risk of expressing them indirectly through anger or internally through illness or depression.

9. **I feel myself joined with God's caregiving team.** See yourself as a caregiver who is never alone, alienated, or separated. Call on God's promise: " ... I will never leave you nor forsake you" (Joshua 1:5). You are continually linked with the true source and center of strength and power. God Himself has made that happen through Jesus Christ.

You certainly will feel the pangs of human isolation at times, but you are not abandoned. You are part of an intricate and holy process of spiritual growth and development that God has set in motion for your own good and for the good of others. The Holy Spirit ties you to His power to enable you to bridge the human needs of your aging parent and your own development.

10. **I feel spiritually stable and steadfast, seeking approval from God alone.** Children want and need approval from their parents, and adult chil-

dren caregivers are no exception. Seeing the role as part of the journey of faith will help you grow beyond earthly approval. You stand firmly on the rock of Jesus Christ who is the love of God, immovable mercy, and hope. "Jesus Christ is the same yesterday and today and forever" (Heb. 13:8). Through Him, you have approval and acceptance in the eyes of God. The Holy Spirit, through Word and Sacrament, will help you remain rooted and resolute as you weather the sometimes stormy times that elder caregiving can generate.

Conclusion

Our feelings move us though the drama of life. We travel at the direction of our feelings. Some of us are the folks who one psychiatrist friend of mine calls "exquisitely sensitive." To have this condition is both an asset and a liability. Being sensitive allows you to deeply appreciate the emotional journey others plod through in their lives; you can be immensely more empathetic and helpful. On the other hand, this sensitivity can nick your heart like a razor. Do it too many times and you begin to bleed to death.

We are charged to deal with our feelings. In order to do this, we must first name them, then we must claim them, and finally, we must proclaim them. This three-step procedure can help you feel what's good and positive about the caregiving role but not get lost in the negative feelings that can paralyze you.

Prayer for Positive Feelings

Dear Lord, take away my feelings of fear and depression and replace them with love and joy. Help me grow in the assurance of Your heavenly guidance and Your tender care. Let me recognize that joy has no cost but that its opposite can be very destructive to me and my relationship with my aging parent. Let me fully grasp that I cannot find joy except in You. This is the joy of eternity that gives me the unified purpose of extending Your love everywhere I go. Bring joy to my heart as I arise in the morning and peace to my soul as my day progresses. This I ask in Your Son's name. Amen.

7

The Decisions of Caregiving

"My food," said Jesus, "is to do the will of Him who sent Me and to finish His work."
John 4:34

Janet, you may recall, decided some months ago to move with her husband into her parents' home. Janet's sister, who lives near her parents, became "burnt-out" with all the elder care responsibilities as her father's Alzheimer's progressed and her mother's demanding dependence grew. Consumed by guilt, Janet persuaded her husband to quit his job so they could move from another state to live with her parents.

Since that time, Janet has felt the strain of care envelop her life. She feels hopelessly trapped by her mother's self-centered ways, frustrated by her inability to change anything, and guilty that she forced her husband to give up his lifestyle for THIS! Add to that a rising tide of resentment toward her mother's apparent lack of appreciation. In her compassionate decision to "rescue" her parents, Janet was naively unprepared to handle this confusion. Now that it threatens to overwhelm her into depression, illness, or worse, Janet doesn't know what to do.

In addition, Janet's husband is confused and upset by what he sees as a contradiction. On the one hand, Janet pushed him to help her inject peace and stability into her parents' lives. Against his better judgment he agreed, and now the very opposite seems to have descended upon her and their marriage. They live in chaos, not peace; they experience only turmoil, not stability. Every day brings new problems but the same reaction—Janet gets upset, is unable to manage her parents, and blames herself for her "failures."

Janet and her husband seem to be juggling a dozen contradictory goals with no central theme. They are swamped with a thousand details of elder care that consume their energy and drown their relationship in a whirlpool of uncertainty. They feel a sense of separation and disunity.

How can Janet turn her world around? What direction can she take? Where is she to go from here?

The Edge of Despair

It is at this edge of despair that real growth and change can transform a life. Function five in the personality is "decision." Decisions signal a time to stop and take a personal inventory of where you are and how you got there. Step five is your opportunity, even your invitation, to change—a time to choose peace instead of chaos and security instead of turmoil and agitation. "How?" you ask. The path may be less rocky than you think.

The first decision is to identify which feelings you are experiencing from step four. Are these feelings the ones you want to experience? If they are not feelings of joy and delight, then you need to decide what thoughts you have given yourself in the third step of thinking/evaluation. Decide whether these thoughts are the ones that are most healthy for you. If not, change them! Decide that you can change, that you indeed *must* change. In choosing change, the only things you have to lose are the sickness-producing feelings you experience in step four. So do you want to decide to continue to feel as you do right now—or would you like to change?

Some current psychologists teach that you must build up your ego, you must be assertive, define your SELF. They preach that, at all costs, you must not be hoodwinked, manipulated, or deluded by others. They perceive the world as a cruel and unjust place that should either be avoided if you're weak or conquered if you're strong. Such thinking breeds a sense of separation, making you feel either inferior to those you perceive as stronger than you or superior if you see other folks as less than you. In either case, you delude yourself because you lose sight of your true purpose and goal. Your purpose is to love and your goal is singular—peace of mind. Your struggle then, if indeed it can be called a struggle, is to pursue peace of mind.

It is here, in this philosophical, existential, or spiritual arena, where you find the cloth from which to make your transforming garments. Here is where you find the food to sustain a continuing commitment to those you love. Indeed, it is here where you find the reason and faith to love because here you decide what you really want. The power of choice is yours. Use it as you wish.

The fifth function of the personality, the decision function, can be described in many ways. Here are some words and phrases that may help you better understand this function. All decisions include strategies … options … goals … objectives … priorities … determinations … plans … commitments … choices … resolutions … elections … selections

... preferences ... taking a stand ... insisting upon ... and adopting a vision.

Disempowering Decisions of Chaos

The following 10 choices are disempowering decisions because they bring only turmoil, chaos, and despair to the adult children who abdicate their power of will. In doing so, they align themselves with the chaotic world rather than aligning it with the will of God.

Adult children caregivers who lack choice discretion often ...

1. **Find themselves saying yes when they want to say no.** No can be the most beautiful word in the English language. It is the only word that clearly establishes boundaries. It demarcates the limits of behavior in any given situation. Actually, no is as positive as it may seem negative because in saying where one cannot or will not go, it declares where one can and should go. When negative emotions motivate caring adult children, they want to say no but find themselves saying yes. In doing so, they forfeit their free wills to the whims of their aging parents. The one clear message this gives to aging parents is that their own children aren't supposed to use rational thinking in their dealings with them. When rational thinking is discarded in the relationship, nothing remains to discern whether a parent's

whim is a need or a whimsical desire. This leaves both the adult child and the aging parent floundering, and the relationship is out of control.

2. **Overcommit themselves.** Adult children caregivers have a tendency to place the needs and the wants of their aging parents before their own. They seem to have no yardstick to measure whether any particular action is good, or right, or necessary, or even healthy for their parent. If the parent wants something, then it is the responsibility of the adult child to see that it happens no matter how illogical or unnecessary these wishes may be. In the words of one adult child, she "gave (her)self away until (she) was all used up." As they constantly seek the responsibility of and for their aging parents, adult children caregivers can easily neglect responsibility to and for themselves and their families.

3. **Overreact to changes they can't control.** Because there is so little order and organization to their decision making, adult children seek to impose control over situations where control may not be necessary or even possible. They fear that no one else is there to help them with their endeavors so they try to "take charge" by assuming control over the entire world of their aging parents. In extreme cases, adult children may even attempt to control the aging process in their parents by performing "heroic" deeds or by denying their parents' aging altogether.

4. Consistently seek their parents' approval and affirmation. Depending upon the level of healthy functioning in their family of origin, adult children may act in ways reminiscent of three-year-olds. If the family of origin could be considered seriously dysfunctional, the children received confusing "love messages" from their parents: "I love you very much, but go away" or "You're not worth much, but you better take care of things around here." The children grew up with a confused self-image about who they were and what they were supposed to do. Now this insecurity pushes them to seek approval from their aging parents because they lack the full internal message that "I'm okay."

5. Choose to avoid the entire topic of aging and therefore don't understand the central goal of aging. Erik Erikson, a noted psychological developmentalist, asserts that the central life task of aging is what he called "integrity vs. despair." An older person, said Erikson, will constantly bring up memories in an attempt to fit all the various pieces of the past into a meaningful whole. Memories rise to their conscious mind and beg to be integrated. Erikson says the better an older person is able to integrate the past, the happier this person will be. Those who can not integrate large portions of their lives into an orderly purpose will have the most difficulty in growing old. These persons, Erikson says, will enter despair.

There are two categories of older persons that cannot affirm the central question "Has my life been meaningful and purposeful?" These are the chronically depressed and the persistently angry (cantankerous). These two groups present special problems. The angry feel that their lives have not been meaningful, and it's everyone else's fault (especially the adult child caregiver). Chronically depressed parents feel that it is their own fault, and they never seem to miss an opportunity to express it. Angry older persons externalize their despair while depressed older persons internalize it. Both reactions are pathological.

6. **Don't know how to decide what to do about the very strong negative emotions they feel regarding their aging parents.** Children are supposed to love and honor their parents. What are they supposed to do if they feel emotions that run counter to these precepts? An additional complication is that many adult children were raised in families where feelings were taboo—certainly the expression of negative feelings. Should it be strange that adult children have difficulty dealing with negative feelings, especially toward their parents who enforced the rules in the first place?

We employ several psychological tactics in our vain attempts to sweep these negative feelings away. First, we try to project them onto others. Usually we push them off onto someone we love, such as our spouse or our own children. Next, we simply refuse to feel them. Then we become numb and emotionally wooden. Finally, we try to transform them into something they are not by giving them another name, rationalizing them away, or fighting them when we can no longer deny their existence. None of these tactics works for long.

7. **Try to impose their own wills on their aging parents.** Our culture is very controlling and even raw at times. We seem to have the old "dog-eat-dog" mentality or at least the "try-to-beat-the-system" philosophy. We seek to conquer, to overcome, to influence, or to subdue what we believe opposes us. When this value system is carried, even in a small way, into the adult child/aging parent relationship, the results can be disastrous. The aging parents will resist however they can, and the adult children will become frustrated and try all the harder to impose their wills onto their parents. This, of course, is not done consciously; rather it's done for the good of the aging parent. The paradox is, of course, that when the adult child tries to do good through sheer strength of will, it's assumed that the desired goal will not be achieved.

8. **Suspend their own power of decision in deference to the wants and needs of their aging parents.** Here is the direct opposite of seven, the

behavioral shadow of the decision made there. When adult children become confused, confounded, alienated, guilty, powerless, or hopeless, they tend to move to extremes. Either they take the posture outlined in seven, seeking to impose their own wills in a controlling and judgmental way, or they abdicate their wills to that of others and become passive victims. They can be docile in the way they undertake this or they can move to detachment, even abandonment. Some adult children will completely pull away, "throw in the towel," take an "I-can't-make-a-difference" attitude, or simply ignore their aging parents. Others fall into a state of hopelessness. They figure nothing can be done so they might as well make the parent as comfortable as possible by giving into their every wish. Neither of these positions is healthy, and eventually, they will crumble under their own weight.

9. **Decide they have no options; they are stuck— trapped.** All seems dark; there is no light anywhere, even at the end of the tunnel. The adult children become sure that their aging parents will outlive them. They feel they have forfeited everything to their aging parents; there is no more of them left. There are no options; all is lost. Here is where the despair of caregiving forces adult children to make some crucial decisions. At this low point, caregivers enter depression, become angry (even lashing out in elder abuse), or use this anger

and despair as energy to seek out community resources.

10. **Judge themselves as failures in the caregiving process.** Blaming, condemnation, and judging—all focused on the self—are the decisions of adult children who have lost the way in the maze of caregiving. Depending on how opinionated and perfectionistic the adult child is, the extent of this self-criticism may be very deep and hurtful. In one adult child caregiver support group, I asked how many people judged themselves inadequate to the caregiving role. Every hand went up! They had made the choice that they were the "bad guys." Mostly they had terrible feelings of guilt and turmoil. They were horrified to realize that, at times, they didn't like their aging parents, that they harbored ill feelings and hateful thoughts toward them. Hence they themselves must be "bad people."

Christian Caregivers Make Empowering Decisions

Christian caregivers make fundamentally different decisions than unclarified decision makers. Caregivers who strive to align their free will with God's will make superior decisions. The real difference is that they actively ask God to guide their decision-making process. No, these caregivers aren't receiving divine revelations, but as they stay close to their God through the Word, worship, and participation in the sacrament, God's Holy Spirit does guide their decision making.

The following list of 10 guidelines for decision making provides a counterpoint to the decisions of chaos.

As an enlightened Christian decision maker ...

1. **Choose truth instead of turmoil.** Whenever you decide to believe in an illusion or deny reality, you create internal turmoil. Truth, however harsh it may seem at first, brings peace. Janet finds herself in constant turmoil because she can't accept the truth about her mother. She nurtures the illusion that her mother can and should be a different person, more understanding and sensitive. Because Janet cannot or will not accept the truth about her mother's egocentric nature, she feeds a fearsome conflict that brings even more controversy and resentment.

2. **Choose to let go ... and let God.** Many times you have heard the admonition, "You just have to learn to let go!" This statement probably leads the list of "things easier said than done." You can easily confuse "letting go" with "not caring." The two are not synonymous. Here is a list of "letting go" ideas gleaned from the World Federation on Alcohol Abuse. These have application for adult children caregivers in need of guidance in decision making.

- To let go does not mean to stop caring. It means I can't do it for someone else.

- To let go is not to cut myself off. It's the realization I can't control another.

- To let go is not to try to change or blame another. It's to make the most of myself.

- To let go is not to care. It's to care about.

- To let go is not to fix. It's to be supportive.

- To let go is not to be in the middle arranging all the outcomes. It's to allow others to affect their destinies.

- To let go is not to be protective. It's to permit another to face reality.

- To let go is not to criticize and regulate anybody. It's to try to become what I dream I can be.

- To let go is to fear less and love more.

Face the fact that you aren't God; you don't control your parent's destiny. God is in control; He personally cares for both you and your aging parent. He cares so much that He gave His only Son as a price for the sin of all people and, in so doing, effected the eternal destiny of every person. And God knows you (and your parent) personally. As part of your "letting go," ask His Spirit to guide you as you meditate on Matt. 10:29–31 and Luke 12:22–34.

3. **Choose relaxation rather than turmoil.** Personal relaxation is another way of seeking peace—both of which are the opposite of turmoil and distress, the core of overcommitment. We live in stressful times, or so we are told. This fact is only compounded when you shoulder the caregiving responsibility. Your need for relaxation and peace seems great. Yet where does peace come from?

Peace comes from God. "But the fruit of the Spirit is love, joy, *peace*, patience, kindness, goodness, faithfulness, gentleness and self-control" (Gal. 5:22). He has made peace with you through Jesus Christ. That is real peace. As you grow in that peace under the guidance of the Spirit, you can decide to make peace and relaxation, not turmoil, your goal in the relationship with your parent.

Janet chooses turmoil each time she sees her mother's requests as demands, each time she evaluates and doesn't accept, each time she chooses fear and separation rather than love and truth.

4. **Choose love instead of fear.** Where there is fear, love cannot shine forth. Where there is love, fear is completely illuminated away. Can you decide to choose between love and fear? Janet chose fear when she decided to live in her mother's house—

for fear her mother would break her hip, set the house on fire, or be forced into a nursing home. Janet can choose love when she admits her powerlessness to control her parents' lives, when she let's go of their destiny. Letting go is very different from abandonment.

Choose love and then choose to grow in love. Once again, God's Spirit working through the Word will help you grow in your love. "There is no fear in love. But perfect love drives out fear, because fear has to do with punishment. The one who fears is not made perfect in love" (1 John 4:18). To help you consider the role of love, meditate on the "love chapter"—1 Corinthians 13.

5. **Choose to strive for a quality, peaceful, emotionally sharing relationship with your aging parent.** You can honor your aging parent the most by building a quality relationship. A quality relationship is characterized by "being with" the parent emotionally (regardless of geography) not "doing for." Love is more clearly demonstrated by support than by trying ceaselessly to find "solutions." There are no solutions to aging. Try to focus on what you do right rather than what went wrong.

6. **Choose peace of mind instead of chaos.** With peace of mind as your primary goal, you are free to let go of all the conflicting goals that confound your

life. Out of guilt Janet chose to move in with her mother. Guilt, fear, and loneliness are never positive reasons to act; they can only bring pain. Janet probably would have made a very different decision had she chosen peace of mind as her motivation.

Peace is different from harmony-seeking. If your only goal is to keep the waters calm, you postpone the inevitable pain of feeling trapped. Seeking harmony in this fashion is simply pleasing others rather than truly loving yourself in a Christian sense. Seeking internal peace requires that you first know yourself and grow in understanding of God's love for you as His child.

7. **Choose that God's will be done ... not your will or your parent's will, or anyone else's.** God's will is the only reality there is. If your plans, your goals, and your motivations are not reflections of God's will, then they only can be your interpretations of what the world teaches. Many adult children find it very difficult to let go ... they want control, not for any reasons of power mongering, but because they truly believe that theirs is the best way. Because you think your plan is the best, you try to impose it on your aging parent—usually with disastrous consequences. Janet's parents will age according to God's plan and not Janet's or her parents' plan anyway. Again, ask for God's Holy Spirit

to help you understand His plan, His will in your caregiving role. Quietly and gently, when you listen, the answer will be given. Be prepared to "hear" answers that may not be what you expect or even want.

8. Choose joy and not guilt. To be joyous means you are at peace in knowing that your actions are consistent with your beliefs. When they are not, you feel guilt because you think you have not measured up to your own or someone else's expectations. At times your parent's expectations (needs, wants, desires) do not represent reality in the sense that they are not genuinely necessary. This means that you may, in fact, be feeling a sense of guilt as a consequence of illusionary—not real—expectations.

Janet feels a continuous sense of painful guilt. She feels as though she cannot and will never meet the "wants" (expectations) her mother demands of her. If Janet could recognize her mother's demands as the desperate attempts of a forlorn woman to gain some control over her world, perhaps she would be more understanding, and yet more realistic, in her interactions with her mother.

9. Choose God's plan not the world's plan. Choosing God's plan is to choose peace; choosing the world's is to find agony and emptiness. God is full and fulfilling for Janet. When her mother demands that Janet make her a cup of tea, or answer the phone, or clean her body (even though her mom is capable of doing these things for herself), Janet has the choice of saying as the world would, "Get it yourself. You're not a cripple." However, she can choose an alternate path and respond with something like, "Mom, I feel so manipulated when you ask me to do things that you might try to do for yourself. Do you think you might be able to try to do this by yourself next time?" God's presence in your heart will be reflected in your body, and it will make a positive difference.

God promises us that He will light our way through trials. You can choose to see His light in every situation by asking yourself, "What would Christ do in this case?" You'll be surprised at the gentle unfolding of illumination you'll encounter when you start to do this and when you pray for His guidance. Otherwise the darkness of the world will be your only companion and confusion your only friend. When you let God's light in, darkness automatically disappears.

10. **Choose love and trust rather than blame and condemnation.** Self-condemnation seldom comes in its most direct and raw form of outright self-hatred. Rather it creeps into your heart in "self-talk," which usually begins with "I should ... ." Such self-

talk is implicitly condemning because it relegates you to a position of fault. You are saying that you are the cause of something evil or the prevention of something good. In either case, your self-berating serves to diminish you personally and negate you spiritually.

Choosing love and trust is not easy. You need to learn to love yourself—and that grows out of learning to trust God as the true loving Father who forgives your sins in Jesus Christ. Look to His Word and the guidance of the Holy Spirit, for the promise is clear: "God demonstrates His own love for us in this: While we were yet sinners, Christ died for us" (Rom. 5:8). As a child of God, you will make mistakes by commission and omission, yet He forgives. If He promises to forgive you, you can learn to forgive yourself.

Conclusion

Decisions are made from a series of options that are based on your priorities, goals, and objectives. From these, you decide the strategies you will use to achieve these goals. Decisions represent what you have decided you want. Decisions convert dreams and possibilities into potential action. Decisions are like headlights on your car on a dark night—without them you can't go very far safely.

Prayer for Powering Decisions

Dear Lord, help me to recall that decision making is a power that I do have. Give me the strength to make powerful decisions and the faith to decide with You always. Let me remember that I cannot make powering decisions by myself but only with You—You are the power in my decisions. Every decision I make defines who I am; help me make decisions knowing that I am Your child through the redeeming work of Jesus. In His name. Amen.

8

Christian Action in Caregiving

Now that I, your Lord and Teacher, have washed your feet, you also should wash one another's feet. John 13:14

Harriet came into my office suffering from a curious sense of agitated anger. She began to unfold the story of how her mother (now 80 years old) had come to visit 15 months ago and never left. The visit was to be a postrecuperative time after her broken hip and rehab in her home city some 450 miles away. However, the visit had somehow turned into a permanent arrangement. Harriet's emotional stability was now twisted to the breaking point.

Harriet's story was complex. She had one sibling, an older brother who lived on the West Coast.

Harriet had shouldered the primary caregiving role, making 11 plane trips to see Mother the year she broke her hip. Harriet got the phone calls in the middle of the night when her mom felt increased pain. Harriet played the mediator between Mother and her doctor, her pharmacist, her minister, her neighbors, the utility companies, and her landlord.

Despite this, Harriet reported oppressive criticism from her mother. Her mom could let nothing go by, making negative comments about virtually every facet of Harriet's life. Harriet's only escape was to vacate her own home at every chance. Yet this criticism was not new; she and her mother had always shared a relationship best described as a "conflicted coalition." They were locked in a mutually damaging emotional hold.

Harriet's response was equally virulent attacks and rebuffs of her mother. Mother and daughter seemed unable to retreat from the battleground. While professing emotional exhaustion, Harriet would confess her equally unshakable drive to "get back" at her mother. She was rationally grasping all of this but was emotionally helpless to let go of her destructive behavior.

Together we analyzed her situation and found some interesting facts that could shed light. Harriet's father died when she was a child. Soon afterwards her brother left for college, leaving her to deal with her mother. Always a dependent, demanding woman, her mother's basic emotional posture was now overlaid with bitter reaction over losing her husband. Instead of creating an emotional counterbalance by becoming compliant, (the dutiful "good daughter" model, which is the most common reaction in such situations), Harriet became a "resistive, contrary daughter." In a sense, Harriet met fire with fire.

———◆———

There could be several reasons why Harriet adopted the counterpoint position. First, she could be angry that her mother wasn't like the other neighborhood moms. This anger explodes when Harriet tries to control the uncontrollable in her mother. Her mother will not change, instead becoming more crystallized by Harriet's counter-criticism.

Second, Harriet could be angry that her present life has been so disturbed by her mother's presence. As a result, she actively retaliates against her. When she is in the same room with her mother, Harriet says her "skin crawled" with contempt.

Third, she could have internalized her mother's criticism. The consequence of this would be to devalue herself and thus develop low self-esteem.

In its extreme form, such a definition might force Harriet, in some contorted way, to believe she needs to be punished. Maintaining a struggle with her mom ensures that the verbal punishment from her mother continues.

Finally, the explanation that I chose as most likely was that Harriet is using her mother because she is fearful of taking her next life steps. As a widow of four years, Harriet has yet to enter the world of work. She wants to but blames her mother for preventing her. But Harriet had made no preparation toward returning to work. In addition, she is dating a man whom she elevates to near angelic proportions. In reality, Harriet feels inadequate to sustain a lasting relationship with him. Again she blames her mother: "How can he want a permanent relationship with a woman who has her live-in mother to care for?"

What had first appeared as a dreadful trap emerges as an unconscious attempt by Harriet to control her life. Her own fear seems to push her to this excessive behavior, controlling not only her mother but her own destiny as well. Harriet needs liberation, not so much from her mother, but from the extremely controlling behavior she has adopted as her norm.

Action: Personality Function Six

Your action is the sixth function of personality. Action is behavior you choose to perform as a result of the other five functions of your personality. Back in chapter seven, Janet wasn't forced to make tea for her mother, nor was she forced to bang her fist on the kitchen counter, nor stuff her feelings down her own emotional pipe. Each of these actions happened as a result of her beliefs, perceptions, thoughts, feelings, and decisions. Her behavior, however erratic, was not random. The action can be viewed as the logical (if not rational) extension of what came before it in Janet's world.

You cannot *NOT* take action as a consequence of your feelings and decisions ... some action will take place. The question is, will it be automatic action or will it be an action of your deliberate and conscious choice? Your actions are consequences of your previous stages. The more you are conscious and aware as you move through the stages, the more satisfying and successful the action you take. Would you rather take action of your own design or action that just happens?

Some ways to describe action, the sixth function of the personality, would be: obeying rules ... failures ... successes ... responses ... reactions ... outcomes ... consequences ... addictions ... accepting

... performances ... serving ... operating ... practice ... accomplishments ... labor ... and all exercising of one's gifts and talents.

Ten Disempowering Caregiving Actions

Adult children caregivers with fragmented actions tend to ...

1. **Suffer from physical and emotional pain and believe it's the normal "sacrifice" of caregiving.** Sometimes our Christian heritage distorts the notion of sacrifice into a positive action: "If I feel pain, this must be a sacrifice, and that's good for my soul." Such ideas spawn the kind of physical and emotional suffering that some adult children endure as their behavioral dues, prostrating themselves before the sacrificial altar of elder caregiving. I've gathered several quotes from very caring yet "righteously" suffering caregivers.

   > "I did experience some physical problems during the time when Mother broke her pelvic bone and then went into the hospital. I had sleeplessness, my thyroid stopped functioning, some bowel inconsistency, and irregular shoulder pain."

   > "Tension headaches—physical or emotional?"

   > "Lately I have more depression than physical pain. I see Mom almost every day and feel depressed afterward. And I was one who never

got depressed. I've been thinking lately to just see her once or twice a week ... but ... ."

"Recently I spent eight months caring for my father in his home. I did so until I could no longer lift him in and out of bed. My back discomfort was intense. My father is now in a nursing home. I am dealing with my feelings about the change. I seem to receive the brunt of his anger, more so than the other brothers and sisters."

"Energy level is used up all the time."

2. **Blame their aging parents unmercilessly.** Harriet could not stop blaming her mother. Truth and reality had little to do with the barbs of malice Harriet jabbed at her mother. Yet we find these criticisms, on both sides, are only means of diffusing other fears. Her mother is fearful of being alone while Harriet is fearful of addressing the developmental tasks in her own life. Each is trapped in her own fear and anger. And the battle will rage as long as each needs the other in those negative ways!

3. **Undervalue themselves, their worthiness, and their innate lovableness.** Insecurity seems to follow some adult children around like a shadow. They see themselves as ineffective and, worse yet, as uncaring and inadequate. They feel like failures, never doing the "right" action, thinking everyone else is right or, at least, "better." They repeat the

same self-criticism, taking little slices of themselves with each swipe of the blade of self-condemnation. Their self-concept as a caregiver is abysmal, their self-confidence is easily shattered, and their belief in their ability to take caregiving actions is confused. Naturally, they are "chasing their tails" in a frenzy of discordant activity.

4. **Become stuck in a habitual, even crystallized, mode of caregiving action.** Once adult children decide that no change can come about in the relationship with their aging parents, a certain resignation creeps in, causing their caregiving to become rigid. This is summed up dramatically by a resigned caregiver.

> "In many respects, I deal with my aging parents as I would deal with a stranger—humane, kind, and sympathetic but without love. Approximately 10 years ago, I finally accepted the reality that I was never going to receive the love I wanted from my parents. With that, I stopped trying to please and began looking to meet my needs. I continue to communicate with my aging parent and care for her physical needs, such as doctor's appointments, food, clothing, etc., but I have separated myself from her emotionally."

Another adult elder caregiver became stuck because she didn't know what else to do.

"Four years ago, I brought my dad here from an eastern state. Nine months earlier, he had had a massive stroke and was permanently paralyzed on his right side, unable to walk, talk, read, or write. Six weeks later, my mother died of cancer, and I have had my dad since then. He lives in my home.

"When I read your description of the attitudes that terrorize adult children, I thought you must have been secretly following me around, cataloging all my feelings, emotions, and the daily dilemmas I face alone. My siblings won't help me, and my children are antagonistic about my father's presence in our home. I cannot bring myself to put him in a nursing home ... I employ a nursing aide to care for my dad while I teach elementary school. I care for him in the evenings, weekends, and all summer. I realize I am burning my candle at both ends, but I don't feel there are any acceptable solutions to my situation. I am always tired, sometimes irritable, and often somewhat depressed."

5. Compulsively do, do, do ... When feeling sorry for their aging parents—especially when a medical condition keeps them from enjoying life—the adult children can make promises of care and personal presence in heroic proportions. Soon the promises seem absurd, if not simply unrealistic. The children begin to feel used, overwhelmed, and confused. Still the caregivers see no other options but to keep doing, doing, doing.

6. Act as "superpersons," behaving as though their assistance can actually change the aging process itself. In some cases, when the adult children see that their work is not making things better, they will try doing more not less. And the cycle goes on. This is actually ceaseless striving designed to alter the course of the normal developmental process called aging. Sooner rather than later, but almost universally, adult children caregivers become disillusioned when the weight of reality is simply too heavy to deny any longer. The caregivers move from confusion to anger (with all its attendant emotions of guilt, fear, and bitterness) and then to depression. It's in the depression phase that these valiant caregivers find their way to my counseling office. Some go to their physicians with symptoms as varied as their personalities.

7. Become continuously "on guard"—alert and vigilant, surveying their aging parents. Adult children can fixate on the needs and wants of their aging parents. Some suffer from "thought stoppage" where thoughts about their parents crowd everything else from consciousness. There is a clear compulsion to their mental activity—alert to every possible change, every potential variation from the way things were yesterday. It's as though they have mentally taken over their parents' lives.

8. Give up in the face of mounting responsibili-

ties. The opposite of seven is giving up. Giving up is very different from letting go. Giving up means the decision has been made (consciously or unconsciously) not to take any action when some form of action might be possible. Giving up is not to be confused with abandonment. Giving up is when caregivers cease to call their aging parents, when they don't seek care for their parent's depression as quickly as they might, when conversations with their parents become recitations of what they need to do rather than exchanging ideas and feelings. Giving up creeps into the relationship quietly.

Many adult children focus on the physical setting of the caregiving role, i.e. food, clothing, and shelter. They quit trying when they realize that everything possible has been done on the physical level or that their parents refuse to change anything. It may not occur to them that the real test of a caregiving role is the quality and depth of the relationship between parent and child. One can never give up on the relationship.

9. **Become sick as a direct consequence of dealing with their aging parents.** Adult children of aging parents are persons "at risk" for sickness and emotional upset because of the increased stress caused by their caregiving role. They are also "at risk" for aging before their time. The proximity to the chronic ailments of their parents, plus sometimes toxic interactions between them, can press adult care-

givers into a posture of negative emotions and premature aging.

Perhaps the most damaging attitude that leads to sickness is that the caregivers become so concerned with the "wants" of their parents that they suspend all that is healthy for themselves. This is not honoring one's mother and father; one cannot honor one part of God's creation by dishonoring another. When one's own needs are suspended, ill health in some form cannot be far behind.

10. **Live a spiritually ungrounded life.** Adult children caregivers can lose their faith, trust, and hope in God as a consequence of the caregiving role. It's not that they abandon the church or stop participating in the activities of their religion. Instead they lose their spiritual heart; their relationship with God becomes so clouded by the strain of care that they slowly lose sight of their center, their source of strength. They drift, becoming ever more vulnerable to emotional storms and affective tides.

Empowering Christian Actions of Caregiving

When you are connected to God, your actions tend to ...

1. **Use acceptance as a central theme of caregiving.** Harriet perceived the problem as her mother's doing. Her first step in fixing her dilemma is to "own" the situation as her problem. Then she can

also claim it as her challenge and vehicle for growth. In a study of caregivers, I found that they identified acceptance as their number one need. Is Harriet accepting her mother, her decision, her feelings, her history, her deficits? You need to fully accept the reality of aging, its consequences for you and your parent, and your powerlessness in the face of these realities.

Note the striking paradox in the first of the 12 steps of the Alcoholics Anonymous (AA) philosophy. The first step asserts that "I am powerless over alcohol ... ." How can claiming powerlessness help the alcoholic triumph over or grow through the disastrous effects of abusing alcohol? One would think the opposite to be true. In some curious fashion, by admitting to your inherent powerlessness to change your aging parent—to let go of your attempts at controlling—you can transcend the attempt to find solutions. In so doing, you find a sense of peace among the negative emotions, including suffering and sacrifice, which formerly overran your countenance.

2. **Offer your aging parent your complete, unconditional, and loving forgiveness.** Forgiveness means recognizing your parent did not harm you. It's true that some well-intended love somehow gets expressed in rather hurtful ways, but still the epicenter of your parent's motivation is love, not

hurt. You may find it hard to swallow, but wasn't all the discipline you received as a young child really designed for your own good? Wasn't it then a form of love, regardless of the perception you had at the time? Could your parent's current behavior be generated from the same motive? It may be hard to believe, but give it some thought.

Forgiveness is the mainstay of your program to produce peace in your life. Forgiveness is your path to peace because the opposite can only bring pain. Grudges, feuds, and interpersonal tension of all kinds are the result of judging. Forgiveness cuts through all of this and provides you with the restful knowledge of being in harmony with God, who forgives you in Jesus Christ. Harriet could transform her entire relationship with her mother if she could assert the personal principle of withholding judgment.

3. **Celebrate the absolution God grants you in the death and resurrection of His Son and ask His help in forgiving yourself.** God knows that there is no perfection, that there is sin in this world. Sin—that's what it is when you try to control your own destiny (or that of others) and try to put yourself in control. That's why God took human form in the being of His Son, Jesus Christ, and carried the punishment of sin.

But if we walk in the light, as He is in the light, we have fellowship with one another, and the blood of Jesus, His Son, purifies us from all sin. If we claim to be without sin, we deceive ourselves and the truth is not in us. If we confess our sins, He is faithful and just and will forgive us our sins and purify us from all unrighteousness. 1 John 1:7–9

As you work at forgiving yourself, take your lead from God's Word and His forgiveness for you. First, confess. Identify what you have done wrong to yourself. Second, repent, that is, tell yourself you don't want to do it again and that you'll work to change so you won't do it again. Third, believe that you can receive forgiveness. Finally, absolve yourself. In effect say (do it aloud), "You're forgiven; go and sin no more."

4. **Actively seek change—ways of making your caregiving relationship better.** An insightful adult child caregiver talked about her aging mother who lived alone some 40 miles away. She outlined the "craziness" of approaching her caregiving responsibilities in exactly the same way as she always had. She was making the same mistakes over and over again. She didn't exactly know what these mistakes were, but she was open to exploring possibilities.

She explained that she needed to look at her

mother and her caregiving role with "new eyes." This was not a denial of reality, she reasoned, but indeed a means of perceiving reality more clearly and accurately than she had—to be more accepting of what was true. She wanted to do things in a different way, to adopt a new sense of "yielding." The way she was running her life, she argued, was simply not working. What she related seemed to be giving greater definition and certainly practical meaning to the whole notion of creative acceptance.

5. **Create a quality, peaceful, emotionally sharing relationship with your aging parent.** Establishing a quality caring relationship with your aging parent is one of the most important tasks you will undertake. As I stated in the last chapter, you honor your aging parent the most by trying to build such a relationship. It is characterized by emotionally "being with" rather than physically "doing for." You will more clearly demonstrate your love for your parent as you support her rather than always attempt to find "solutions." Remember, there are no solutions to aging. Focus on what you are doing right in your relationship with your parent rather than what may have gone wrong.

Creative acceptance demands a live-in-the-present attitude, which is implicitly positive. Once experienced, it is seen as natural and normal rather than artificial and awkward. Acceptance brings with it an inner peace, an eternal calm that feels like a piece of heaven. It's comforting and affirming, trusting and loving.

Creative acceptance helps you transcend the fear that you are somehow losing something because of your caregiving role. Acceptance helps you see what you have gained through your caregiving. When you perceive caregiving as a loss, it engenders a split mind and necessarily brings strident resistance and emotional turmoil. View caregiving as a learning process and, therefore, a path toward growing and gaining, and you will be more able to be in harmony with God's will for you.

6. **Come to deeply trust in God to maintain your peace of mind.** Coming to terms with aging and its effects requires a certain amount of personal surrender; trying to control aging will likely bring its opposite—chaos. This of course seems paradoxical. The best way to gain control is to give up the notion that control is possible and simply "let go."

Sometimes it seems that we can only trust things to go wrong. To counteract this perception, it's imperative that you trust deeply that what is happening is governed by God. No, God does not allow suffering for its sake alone. A larger growth process is occurring here, and it has far-reaching consequences. How easy it is for Janet to blame her mother for her sharp and abrasive personality. She even lapses into figuratively shaking her fist at God, blaming Him for the pain and "senseless" suffering she feels and sees in her mother. Blame and trust are at opposite ends of the spectrum. Blaming always brings a repercussion of fear while trust brings peace—a peace Janet needs desperately.

7. **Seek contact with God through prayer and His Word for the knowledge of God's will and the power to put that will into practice.** This is a paraphrasing of the tenth step in the AA philosophy. You are not in control of your own parent's aging process, and you cannot act as though you are! Nor does your aging parent have control over his own aging. This control is out of your hands. When you are in contact with God through prayer and His Word, you are surrendering control into God's hands.

Adult children caregivers who are striving to learn from the changing relationship between themselves and their aging parents use words such as "surrender," "distance," "disengage," "detach," "noninterfere," "let go," and "let it be" to describe their emerging posture with their aging parents. Again we see a paradox. As this disengagement process proceeds, the love and closeness between parent and child become more clear and enriching. Together, these give you an expanded understanding of a process where you maintain yourself by perceiving the events of your life differently. As you perceive differently, you eventually feel, decide, and act in ways more in keeping with objective reality.

The obvious spiritual theme running through acceptance is underscored by the fact that you need to exercise faith.

8. **Dedicate yourself to doing God's work by helping others in the same distress you formerly found yourself.** Here again is a paraphrasing of the twelfth step of AA. One clear way of moving beyond negative resignation, or giving up, is to help others. You need other caregivers for support and information. This can best happen in a support group. I have been privileged to facilitate such a group for the past 10 years. So many people have come into the group with fear and guilt layered over themselves like armor. It's so enriching to see the plates of fear and guilt slide from their shoulders as they learn that they are not "bad," rather they are simply people who have become lost seeking better ways to love. This is the message of a support group. When you are freed of the chains that bind you to your negative thinking, you are motivated to help others who find themselves in

the same predicament. The flow of love continues. And as love is extended, it comes back in greater abundance.

9. **Become challenged by the caregiving role not defeated by it.** Caregivers are quick to point out that moving from a posture of control to one of acceptance is not tantamount to defeat. Indeed the contrary is true: They regard this transformation as a challenge. They find this nonresistant stance to be in harmony and accord with the central learning task of aging—that of developing integrity. This brand of integrity speaks to wholeness, completeness, and cohesiveness as opposed to fragmentation, separation, and brokenness. Controlling begets illness and loss of self. Acceptance fosters health and self-preservation. Acceptance confers a power to handle the conflicting negative emotions your caregiving role often brings.

10. **Become grounded in virtue (love in action) as the guiding principle for your caregiving endeavors.** Elder caregiving is tough. In many ways it can be the most frustrating and demanding endeavor you will ever encounter. Without the light of love as your guiding torch, elder caregiving can be a dark, frightening, never-ending road that leads to nothing but death. The road signs along the way are guilt, helplessness, anger, fear, and resentment. There is little or no respite along this road, no way station or

rest stop, only the incessant push of the need for care, every day, every day ... every day.

You can so easily overlook the volume of altruistic, virtuous things you do every day. Instead you focus on the very few times you forgot and made a mistake. These "mistakes" in caregiving are many times simply a sharp glance, an unkind word, an untoward thought or feeling, a slight deceit, or some small omission or oversight of responsibility. The point is, don't overlook the times you do practice virtues.

You can only know virtues by actually practicing them not by defining them or talking about them. Virtues are beyond knowledge. Instead they are only known through experience, and experience progressively achieved leads to wisdom. The practice of virtues generates ever greater levels of virtue. In your day-to-day life, virtue is realized by consistently choosing the most healthy path. As you become more proficient at choosing, you develop your moral character, which, in turn, allows you to experience virtues even more. You have no lack of choices to make in your work with your aging parent and, therefore, have many opportunities to practice virtues.

The Top Elder Caregiving Virtues

In a study I conducted on virtue practices among

adult children caregivers, the following were identified as most needed for success in the caregiving role. They are listed in the order of their importance as rated by caregivers themselves.

1. Acceptance—the act of being nonjudgmental.
2. Strength—capacity for exertion or endurance.
3. Peace—a state of tranquility or quiet.
4. Patience—bearing pains or trials calmly or without complaint.
5. Hope—expectation of fulfillment or success.
6. Self-control—restraint exercised over one's own impulses, emotions, or desires.
7. Joy—the state of happiness; a source or cause of delight.
8. Harmony—internal calm.
9. Gentleness—mildness of manners or disposition.
10. Love—committed to giving what one needs. Unselfish loyal and benevolent concern for the good of another.

Conclusion

Your actions are the crowning function of your personality. You are the one who chooses to either react or to respond. When you react, you follow the directives of the world, doing what comes naturally to the world. You invest very little thought, discernment, or introspection. You don't invite God to take His rightful place in your process of understanding the situation. Consequently, you bow to the precepts of the world and find your "reward" in the things of this world that are always grounded in fear, guilt, and anger.

You are called to *respond* rather than react. When you respond, you do so in full knowledge and appreciation of the five functions of the personality that came before. Before you take any action, you scan through the previous five functions, searching the theme of the movement through the five. Did you include God in all steps along the way? Are you acting in accordance with His will? Can this action lead to greater peace between you and your aging parent? Is your action listed in the first 10 disempowering actions or in the second list of 10 powering actions? The choice is yours to make; the consequences are always either of this world or of God!

Prayer for Powering Action

Dear Lord, please be at my side as I move through this earthly journey. Walk with me as I make the choices for action with my aging parent. Let me rest with You awhile as I prepare myself for the next move I will be asked to make with my aging parent. Help me not lose sight of You as I act, sometimes in quick succession. Help me, dear Lord, respond as

You would have me respond and to overlook the much more enticing choices the world offers me. Assist me to act in ways consistent with Your will, and not my own. In Jesus' name. Amen.

9

Putting It All Together: Using Christian Personality Powering in Caregiving

Nancy held her head in her hands. She had spent the last 36 hours in the intensive care waiting room, clutching every word of encouragement the nurses and doctors could give concerning her mother's condition. Her mother had had a stroke, and she was now paralyzed on her left side and couldn't talk. How painful for Nancy to look into her mother's seeking and terrified eyes, knowing she was straining to communicate ... in vain. Nancy couldn't think of a more horrible feeling than not being able to talk when you were as scared as her mother was now.

So many thoughts and memories had raced through Nancy's mind during the past 36 hours. She thought of how Mom had struggled the time Dad lost his job ... how she delighted in the births of Nancy's children ... and how ready she seemed to be when Nancy needed help with child care or just a shoulder to lean on. Mom really was a wonderful woman ... she had her faults, but this poor, struggling human being was her mother ... and she was so helpless now.

If there was ever a time Mom needed her, Nancy reasoned, it was certainly now!

Feeling Sorry

There were two weeks of healing for her mother in the hospital. She had regained some movement on her left side and was even able to form certain words. The social worker cautioned Nancy that her mother required much care, perhaps too much for her to handle. However, Nancy wanted nothing but to have Mom come live with her. Her mother had lived alone since Dad died eight years ago. Certainly she couldn't care for that house anymore, and Nancy couldn't stand the thought of having people in to care for her—or, worse yet, putting Mom in a nursing home.

Heroic Acts of Caregiving

Nancy withdrew from her volunteer position and quit the part-time sales job she had enjoyed for five years. She rearranged her sleep schedule because Mom required medication every four hours. Meals were vastly different now because Nancy fed her mother. Her social life required modification because Nancy couldn't seem to find a "parent sitter" when she and Herb (her husband) wanted to go out. But when Nancy looked into her mother's longing eyes, she would feel so fulfilled knowing she was somehow returning the care that her mother had given her.

Confusion

The doctor said Mom was actually quite healthy. However, she would not regain any more movement or speech. Nancy was devastated! It was now four months since the stroke. The news seemed to pierce Nancy's heart. She had so many conflicting feelings, but the strangest was the resentment she was feeling now—as if Mom was responsible for being ill. How could this be? She was giving Mom such good care ... why wasn't she getting any better? It didn't seem right. Her brother and sister called often to get the latest information about Mom's condition. Now these phone calls seemed annoying after being so welcome, even comforting, in the past. Something strange was happening, and Nancy was confused.

Anger and Resentment

Weeks dragged into months, and the fleeting sense of resentment now seemed to crystalize into rather substantial spells of anger. The question "Why is my own mother doing this to me?" flashed through her mind daily. Rationally, Nancy knew that Mom wasn't doing this deliberately, and yet she seemed to need someone to blame for all the negative feelings swirling inside of her. Nancy's anger would come out in very unproductive ways: sometimes at her husband, sometimes at her siblings, at other times directed at her mother. After all, who else was responsible for making her life this unsatisfying succession of mundane tasks. If all of this failed, she would hold herself in contempt for not being the caregiver that she should be.

Depression

Once her anger was directed at herself, Nancy started becoming depressed. At first the depression took the form of periods of being sad, blue, and down. Next, she noticed a variety of physical symptoms. She couldn't get to sleep when she wanted and awoke early in the morning. She had more stomach problems and more headaches. Life had lost its zest; Nancy had become dull, boring, and unhappy. One day she would have little appetite, and the next she could eat a horse. The natural rhythm and flow of her life seemed to melt away. She couldn't bring herself to laugh.

Steps to Hopelessness

What started as a mission of love for Nancy had brought her to emotional despair. What had forced her to this dismal place—laden with layers of conflicting emotions, none of which she wanted?

Nancy's progression is a very common path for adult children caregivers: (1) Feeling sorry; (2) heroic acts of caregiving; (3) confusion; (4) anger and resentment; and finally, (5) depression. This sequence is duplicated by caregivers who believe they are called by the highest of values to serve their parents. Indeed they are—but the beliefs, perceptions, thinking, feelings, decisions, and consequent actions they bring to the caregiving role are not helpful.

Let's itemize the disempowering personality functions that invaded Nancy. As you read through these, try to see how Nancy stumbled over her own personality. Think about how these same notions may be plaguing you in your quest to honor your aging parent.

Disempowering Beliefs

1. I need to be the perfect adult child.
2. My relationship with my mother needs to remain what it always has been.
3. I need to "do it all" for my mother. I must protect her.
4. My mother's needs come before my own.
5. I need to always be in control.

Inaccurate Perceptions

1. I see my life as revolving around my mother ... I have no life of my own.
2. I overestimate the gravity of the problems that surround me.
3. I see myself as limitless.
4. I see myself as selfish if I do things for myself.
5. I have an image that my mother will eventually change.

Distorted Thinking

1. I think I shouldn't have any negative feelings toward my mother.
2. I think I must fix the situation.
3. I think I am responsible for my mother; it's my fault when things go wrong.
4. I think I'm not good enough.
5. I think I know what's best for my mother.

6. I think my caregiving work is never finished.

Negative Feelings

1. I feel guilty very easily because I think I haven't done enough.
2. I feel sorry for my mother because of the losses she has experienced.
3. I feel low energy, emotionally or physically drained, or fatigued because of all the emotional strain.
4. I feel emotionally paralyzed. I cannot show my true feelings.

Irrational Decision

1. I find myself saying yes when I want to say no.
2. I overcommit myself.
3. I don't know how to decide what to do about the very strong negative emotions I feel.
4. I suspend my own power of decision in deference to the wants and needs of my mother.
5. I judge myself as a failure in the caregiving process.

Discordant Actions

1. I undervalue myself, my worthiness, and my innate lovableness.
2. I become stuck in a habitual even crystallized mode of caregiving action.
3. I compulsively do, do, do ...

4. I act as a "superwoman," behaving as though my assistance can actually change the aging process itself.
5. I become sick as a direct consequence of dealing with my mother.
6. I live a spiritually ungrounded life.

As you can clearly see, Nancy became completely unnerved and entangled in her distorted personality functions. She was unable to shift her personality functions to operate in a more enlightened way; she was stuck in the worldly paradigm. Now that she has identified the distorted and dysfunctional processes, she can focus attention on shifting to the level of the Christian caregiver. She can dedicate each day to a different function of the personality and meditate on the enlightened ways she can modify her personality.

Family of Origin Issues

So often what we learned in our family of origin is transferred to our family of creation. At other times, however, we notice the opposite is true. What we experienced in our family of origin we somehow vow not to bring into our family of creation. The selection of what gets brought in and what is rejected seems an internal, unconscious decision, one that is never made in the open. Rather it is forged over the years of our development. We are indeed products of our family of origin based upon these unknown decisions we make regarding what to include and what to exclude.

Nancy could come to a fuller appreciation of the emotional dilemma she confronts with each visit to her mother if she could thoroughly clarify the characteristics and interaction dynamics of her family of origin. So much of what Nancy is feeling toward her mother now is deeply embedded in her memory and has become an unconscious part of the operational functions of her personality.

Ann's Overburden

Ann stroked her brow as she explained her dilemma with her mother. She was the only daughter of a couple whose relationship was, at best, lopsided and, at worst, dysfunctional and destructive. Ann remembers the care, indeed the over care, that her father gave to her mother throughout their married years. Whatever Mother wanted, he was "right there" to satisfy. "A dear, sweet man," she related, with tears in her eyes and a wistful smile.

During her youth, Ann and her mother "got along," although Ann recalls that her mother was somewhat of a perfectionist. Mother always seemed to have a critical word, a judging gesture, or a blaming look for Ann. "It's not that she was a bad or cruel mother," Ann continues, "but it was very difficult for her to give a compliment, an affirmation, or a positive stroke. I grew up thinking that I somehow never measured up in her eyes."

Ann's father was there to soothe her and tell her how much he thought of her. He was quick with gentle encouragement, supportive gestures, and loving words. There was no question that Ann was "Daddy's girl." All the while, Ann's mother was somehow jealous, a bit threatened by this relationship, and she extracted a price for her discomfort by demanding from her husband and finding fault with Ann. None of this conflict ever rose to the level of actual division in the family, but each member was aware of the turmoil even though they kept silent about it. It seemed just too obvious and yet strangely unreal. "Wasn't every family like this?" Ann asked.

Five years ago, when Ann's father died suddenly, Ann's relationship with her mother dramatically changed. It seemed to Ann that her mother expected her to do everything for her, just as her husband had in the past. It seemed as if Mother expected no break in the rhythm of her life; all would be the same except that, instead of her husband, Ann would now have to contort her life and provide all the services.

Ann relates, "For awhile, that's exactly what I did. Whatever mother wanted, I did for her." Cooking, sewing, and cleaning, all tasks that Father had gradually picked up (even more so since retirement) were to become Ann's. As far as her mother was concerned, Ann was now to assume the full burden of care for her and her home. What confounded Ann was that her mother was quite capable of accomplishing most of her own care. Her body and mind were sound; it was only her critically dependent personality that demanded continual care.

Ann was confused and angry—at herself for taking on the burden and also with her mother for being so demanding. Intellectually, Ann knew she needed to break this unwholesome cycle, but she was incapable of doing so. She felt weak and guilty, worn out and irritated, worried and perplexed. Ann had so many different feelings that she could not sort them out into any rational whole that made sense to her.

As Ann gradually expressed herself to the counselor, she began to realize that her mother probably suffered from dependent personality disorder, which her father had catered to their entire married life. Ann realized that she had been pressed into service of the dependency. What was she to do now?

Disempowering Beliefs

1. Aging brings an end to emotional growth and personal development.
2. I need to be the perfect adult child.
3. I need to "do it all" for my mother. I must protect her.
4. My mother's needs come before my own.
5. My mother must be right (even if she does seem illogical).

Inaccurate perceptions

1. I see my life revolving around my mother ... I have no life of my own.
2. I see my mother giving very little—if any—love and approval that I seek so much.
3. I don't recognize the times when my mother is acting in an unhealthy way—intolerant, abusive, or manipulative.
4. I not only don't see the negative aspects of my mother's personality, but I also don't see the positive side of her personality either.
5. I see myself as limitless.
6. I see myself as selfish if I do things for myself.

Distorted Thinking

1. I think I shouldn't have any negative feelings toward my mother.
2. I think I must obey my mother.
3. I think I must fix the situation.
4. I think I'm not good enough.

5. I think my caregiving work is never finished.

Misdirected Feelings

1. I feel guilty very easily because I think I haven't done enough.
2. I feel sorry for my mother because of the losses she has experienced.
3. I feel neglected—having always wanted my mother's love, but feeling that I never got it the way I needed it.
4. I feel rejected by my mother whenever I don't do what she wishes.
5. I feel low energy, emotionally or physically drained, or fatigued because of all the emotional strain.
6. I feel emotionally paralyzed; I feel I cannot show my true feelings.

Irrational Decisions

1. I find myself saying yes when I want to say no.
2. I overcommit myself.
3. I consistently seek my mother's approval and affirmation.
4. I don't know what to do about the very strong negative emotions I feel.
5. I suspend my own power of decision in deference to the wants and needs of my mother.
6. I have come to the conclusion that I have no options; I am stuck—trapped!
7. I am a failure in the caregiving process.

Discordant Actions

1. I suffer from physical and emotional pain, and yet I believe this is normal for the "sacrifice" of caregiving.
2. I undervalue myself, my worthiness, and my innate lovableness.
3. I have become stuck in a habitual, even crystallized, mode of caregiving action.
4. I compulsively do, do, do ...
5. I act as a "superwoman," behaving as though my assistance can actually change the aging process itself or my mother's personality disorder.
6. I have become sick as a direct consequence of dealing with my mother.

Conclusion

As a spiritually enlightened caregiver, you need to become watchful, not of the behaviors in your aging parent, but of your own (1) dysfunctional beliefs, (2) inaccurate perceptions, (3) distorted thinking, (4) misdirected feelings, (5) irrational decisions, and (6) discordant actions. When you uncover any of these errors in the six functions of your personality, it is your cue to switch into your higher level of functioning, your Christian personality powering. Replace the error with the shining product of love that is your very sustenance. This is the essence of Christian personality powering.

10

The Church: Service Potential Unlimited

It was 10:30 a.m., time for Mary to call her mother's home where the "friendly visitor" from church was scheduled to arrive. Well-trained, the volunteer came every weekday, stayed about an hour, talked with Mom, maybe had a cup of tea, and glanced around the place to ensure everything was in order. Periodically, another volunteer, a handyman, stopped to check if anything needed maintenance. Mary's mom also received a daily meals-on-wheels dinner, again coordinated by the church and delivered by a volunteer.

Once a week, her mom is picked up and taken to church for a wellness seminar and support/discussion group staffed by trained, dedicated volunteers. Her mom can call for transportation from the church's senior adult ministry office when she needs it. There is even a 24-hour emergency phone number with volunteers on call.

The senior adult ministry office at church also offers training in peer counseling for seniors, a "Growing Older Graciously" study group, a support group to give Mary guidance and education for caregiving, a faith autobiography class, a bereavement group, and a discussion group on how to remain young-at-heart and youthful-in-spirit. Virtually any need or service is the domain of the senior adult ministry office—all given in a spirit of care with the underlying theme of spiritual development for a lifetime.

This description is of the church of the future, the church that has taken senior adult ministry seriously and has committed time and budget to the escalating needs of seniors and their families. The resources are available to make this dream a reality; all that's required is a decision on the church's part to undertake organized ministry to seniors.

Churches are the natural and logical infrastructure of care for a population of parishioners and members who are gaining in years. This is the same population that laid the cornerstones, organized the child care, set up the educational structures, headed the evangelism efforts, and gave generously to every fund-raising endeavor. Indeed these older members are the ones who gave their hands to

God's work and provided the very life force of the church.

———◆———

Senior adults ... Still Giving

Senior adults are once again at the center of the church, this time not as the energetic and resourceful "givers" but as the receivers of the care of the church. Their need creates a unique opportunity for the church and also points to the glorious hope of the next life. This aging population, then, still gives to the church but in a much different fashion.

Churches need to begin developing and implementing programs that serve the ones who have served them so well for so long. The aging population is thirsty for the healing waters of ministry that only their church can provide. Their families, too, pressured by economic struggle and pressed by the emotional upheaval of caring for an elder, cry for assistance. Where better to find this help than from the cradle of compassionate understanding—their church.

Volunteers of all sorts need to be recruited, motivated, and trained so they can become the front-line workers in helping older church members thrive and not simply survive. A ready-made work force exists in the church because of the growing number of active retirees. People are retiring earlier and are more vigorous, better educated, more financially stable, and more socially aware than ever before. Retirees need and hunger for productive, purposeful, and personally relevant ways of using their time and talents in service to others. Service to seniors in the church is a natural and life-enhancing means for retirees to become more effective, energetic, and full of joy than ever before. What needs to be done to take advantage of the bright potential this army of immensely capable retirees offers?

Two Requirements

To take advantage of the retiree work force, the church must motivate and train these volunteers. Proper motivation stimulates the workers and provides heightened awareness of the developmental stages associated with aging. Volunteers can find motivation as they realize the important service they are providing and develop unique personal reasons for their involvement.

Retirees who understand that they have a conscious task in life, that they have a mission (and can find instruction to accomplish that mission), are among the healthiest retirees around. Not only is helping older adults sanctioned, even commanded, in our Judeo-Christian tradition, but giving service to another of God's children (regardless of their age) is health enhancing to the service provider. There is something fundamentally uplifting—physically, emotionally, mentally, and spiritually—about helping others.

Medical researchers are now finding scientific proof for what Christians have professed for so long—that giving of oneself is actually a form of receiving. It is not farfetched for a doctor to recommend "helping others" to stimulate maximum health right along with other good health practices such as nutrition, rest, and exercise.

Studies of the aging process have reached a similar conclusion. People who directly assist others, who share themselves openly, are healthier, happier, and live longer, more productive lives. The need for connection and altruism seems to be a central ingredient in our internal health-enhancing system. Helping others seems to strengthen us and helps us become grateful for what we have been given.

In addition to identifying and motivating a senior ministry work force, churches need to develop leaders and provide clear direction for its programs. There are many people willing to help older adults, yet leadership is often lacking. Leaders need not be professionals with advanced degrees. Rather, leaders are those who become committed to discovering training opportunities, possess a compassionate heart, and have a giving soul. They naturally attract others to serve. Leaders are ordinary people who are called by God to undertake extraordinary things in Christ's name.

Programs

Before any ministry to senior adults can be effectively organized and executed, volunteers must be recruited and trained. Good training before implementation of the programs will pay rich dividends for the success of the entire program. It's important that training be done in a professional manner, with adequate advance notice. Present this training as a personal and spiritual development program. Make it crystal clear that participation does not require a long-term service obligation. It simply means participants are interested in developing their personal and spiritual lives.

After training the volunteer staff, the church will need to develop and implement programs that meet the needs of its older adult members. Some programs may already exist such as a meals-on-wheels program, a tape ministry, or regular pastoral shut-in calls. However, the senior ministry of the future should consider including a wide range of programs that meet emotional needs as well as the physical and spiritual ones.

Churches could develop programs that help older adults move toward integrity in aging and away from despair. Such programs would help seniors transform negative personality functions to positive ones. Several support groups could be started to guide seniors as they deal with chronic or terminal illnesses. These groups would focus on God's plan for aging and His help and support through Word and Sacrament.

Equally as important as support groups for seniors are support groups for adult children care-givers. These groups would supply the all-important information and support necessary for successful caregiving. The groups also could provide outreach opportunities into the community as elder care-givers network with one another. The basic discussion guide for such groups would be this book.

Finally the church could develop its own unique approaches to strengthening the spiritual lives of its older adults. Special Bible studies and worship opportunities may be started. A faith remembrance hour could be started to record the reminiscences of earlier times in the church and in the faith lives of senior members.

Conclusion

These are merely suggestions for action in senior

adult ministry. They certainly do not exhaust the variety of possibilities for service to seniors in any congregation. Ask your congregation to look into expansion of its offerings to, with, and by seniors. You may be the eventual recipient of the services offered by a program you encourage now. God speed!